BY THE SAME AUTHOR.

Haste to the Rescue; or Work while it is Day. 18mo. 50 cents.

15,000 copies of this work have been sold in England.

WORKS OF A KINDRED CHARACTER.

The Missing Link; or, Bible Women in the Homes of the London Poor. By L. N. R., Author of "The Book and its Story." 12mo. 75 cents.

25,000 copies have been sold in England.

"The 'Missing Link' supplies a new chapter in the history, not only of Christianity, but of civilization. The book treats of the heathen of St. Giles's instead of the heathen of Madagascar, Makalolo, or it would receive a wider circulation, and create a more vivid interest, than the travels even of a Ellis and a Livingstone."—*London Daily News.*

Life-Work; or, The Link and the Rivet. By L. N. R., Author of "The Missing Link; or, Bible Women in the Homes of the London Poor."

Workmen and their Difficulties. By the Author of "Ragged Homes, and how to Mend them."

English Hearts and English Hands; or, the Railway and the Trenches. By the Author of "Memorials of Captain Vicars." 12mo. 75 cents.

43,000 copies of this work have been sold in England.

"The Memorials of Vicars and these Memorials of the Crystal Palace Navvies are books of precisely the same type, and must not be overlooked. We recognise in them an honesty of purpose, a purity of heart, and a warmth of human affection, combined with a religious faith, that are very beautiful."—*London Times.*

O God, for Christ's sake,

Give the Holy Spirit,

That this Book may be profitable to all who read it;

And advance Thy glory, and the Salvation of Sinners!

Amen.

QUARRY WALK, SHREWSBURY.

FRONTISPIECE.

Annals Rescued. p 49.

ANNALS OF THE RESCUED.

BY THE AUTHOR OF

"HASTE TO THE RESCUE."

Mrs. Julia B. Wightman

WITH A PREFACE BY THE

REV. CHARLES E. L. WIGHTMAN.

"Let us lay aside every weight, and the sin which doth so easily beset us, and let us run with patience the race that is set before us, LOOKING UNTO JESUS."

NEW YORK:
ROBERT CARTER AND BROTHERS,
No. 530 BROADWAY.
1861.

PREFACE.

By the Rev. Charles E. L. Wightman.

The following pages contain the experience of working men once slaves to drink, but now, by the blessing of God on the labours of my dear wife, recovered out of that fearful snare which holds so many strong men bound as with chains of iron.

It was a great and wondrous sight when many of these men first occupied the aisles of St. Alkmond's Church. Some of the ordinary congregation, who happened to sit near them, kindly handed them hymn-books, and pointed out the hymns; and I feel sure that the hearts of many present (as well as my own) bounded with joy and thankfulness that those who once were far off are now brought nigh by the blood of Christ.

Sixty or seventy of those who never frequented any place of worship are now regular in their attendance; and it is peculiarly touching to see some twenty of them kneeling month after month at the table of the Lord.

It is most encouraging to think of the prayer-meetings on Saturday evenings and Sunday mornings, when the members of the Society meet and engage with heart and soul in singing the praises of a reconciled Father, and approach the throne of grace for themselves, their families, for a blessing on the means of grace, and on the ministers of the Word.

The same may be said of the more private meetings for prayer which are held weekly at the homes of various members.

Add to this the word in season now spoken by the members to each other on the things that belong to their peace; also the communicants' meetings, both of men and women, held in alternate weeks, when those who fear God tell what He has done for their souls.

And to all this good the first step was total

abstinence from intoxicating drinks—a practice now happily adopted by above one thousand men, women, and children in this Society alone, the benefit of which is now seen and felt in many a contented and thoughtful heart, and at many a fireside where are to be found plenty, comfort, and peace.

Let none, then, despise or overlook the means which have, under God's blessing, brought about such great and blessed results. but rather help forward such a movement with their hearty sympathy and constant prayers.

AUTHOR'S PREFACE.

ADDRESSED TO THE MEMBERS OF ST. ALKMOND'S TOTAL ABSTINENCE SOCIETY.

My dear Friends,—This little book, which some of you have helped me to write, will go forth into many an English home in this land and abroad; and be read with much interest for your sakes.

Join with me in earnest prayer that it may be profitable to all who read it, and advance the glory of God and the salvation of sinners, for Jesus Christ's sake; and may it open the eyes of thousands to the enormity of *that hindrance* placed—NOT BY GOD—in your path, and that of all working men throughout the realm—a hindrance which once kept some of you, and still keeps thousands, from Christ and eternal life!

I have avoided, except in one or two places, mentioning real names, for reasons obvious to you all.

If you recognise the history of a brother or sister in the affecting incidents so nobly given me by some of you, let it kindle love and sympathy in your hearts for the same.

In conclusion, may God, who has vouchsafed so rich a blessing on our work, keep you and me "looking unto Jesus," and may He grant that we may, one and all, meet together in His presence with exceeding joy!

Your affectionate and sincere friend,

JULIA B. WIGHTMAN.

CONTENTS.

A Lesson worth Learning.

"Ask now the beasts, and they shall teach thee;
And the fowls of the air, and they shall tell thee:
Or speak to the earth, and it shall teach thee;
And the fishes of the sea shall declare unto thee."

JOB, xii. 7, 8.

CHAPTER I.

WHO has not heard of the coral reefs which surround the bright and sunny islands of the South Pacific?

Of all the wonders that old Ocean contains, none are more curious or interesting than the elegant plant-like zoophytes, which, with lovely forms and most richly-varied hues, change their submarine bed into a garden of living flowers, making, indeed, a fairy paradise, such as Southey speaks of in those exquisite lines:—

"It was a garden still, beyond all price,
Yet even it was a place of Paradise.
* * * * *
And here were coral bowers,
And grots of madrepores,
And banks of sponge, as soft and fair to eye
As e'er was mossy bed
Whereon the wood-nymphs lie,
With languid limbs in summer's sultry hours.
Here, too, were living flowers,
Which like a bud compacted,
Their purple cups contracted,
And now in open blossom spread.

Stretched like green anthers many a seeking head,
And arborets of jointed stone were there,
And plants of fibres fine as silkworm's thread;
Yea, beautiful as mermaid's golden hair
Upon the waves dispread!
Others that like the broad banana growing,
Raised their long, wrinkled leaves of purple hue,
Like streamers wide outflowing."

These living forms are rooted by a base of lime to some submarine body.

Let us transport ourselves in thought to their strange dwelling-place, and examine them for ourselves.

Far down beneath the ocean there are masses of rock, many leagues in extent, from 800 to 1000 feet in thickness, the entire work of generations of tiny architects through successive ages, in defiance of the ever-restless waves which dash and foam above them.

Compare with these the most stupendous works of man, and do they not sink into insignificance?

Look at the coral skeleton! It assumes every variety of form; sometimes star-like, at another globular, branched, solid, tubular, or like net-work.

Are you aware that a gelatinous organised substance runs through the whole, or is expanded over the surface of the entire ramified skeleton, which it encloses and secretes?

It is *one compound body.* Yet it is nevertheless

formed of distinct little beings, each of which is a separate polype, or digestive sac, furnished with a mouth surrounded by numerous filaments, or tentacule, contributing its share to the nourishment of the whole body politic with which it is organically united.

Here is a grand lesson of mutual dependence and sympathy, combined with individual action and life!

"This physiological relation," writes the late G. F. Richardson, F.G.S., "occasions remarkable associations and singular groupings among the polypifera; hence the stupendous results obtained from their operations in the seas of intertropical regions, by which the life of the individual is combined with the life of the whole, and the nutriment prepared by each organism is made to contribute to the nourishment of the community of which it forms a part."

Look at the stupendous results of these tiny architects! The secret of success in their unwearied labours is the combined action—the mutual dependence and sympathy.

Have we not cause to hide our faces for very shame when we think that more than eighteen hundred years have passed since our blessed Lord was upon earth, and yet so little progress has been made by that living body the Church of Christ for the spread of the Gospel and the evangelization of the heathen?

Just think, again, of the barrier reefs which run along the north-west coast of Australia for upwards of a thousand miles, and see what miracles *combined action* and *mutual dependence* can enable the lowest form of organised life to effect, amidst the roar of ocean and the violence of its ever-restless waves!

And now, turn to Christendom in its best aspect. Look at our highly favoured country, for instance.

Where is the bulwark cast up by combined Christian effort to keep out ignorance and heathenism from our people?

Where is the parish of any size, that does not contain many precious souls, hitherto inaccessible to the pastor by that one fiend, *strong drink?* Men and women, who have grown up, generation after generation, in the midst of us, unknown and unsought,—nay, more, unsought and unsaved!

And now, it is too late to erect a barrier-reef to keep off the ever-restless waves of infidelity and ignorance from approaching the masses; they have done so too long, drifting myriads of human beings annually to the shores of a lost eternity.

We have now to deal with facts as we find them. But it is not too late, blessed be God! to see what love and sympathy, together with combined Christian effort, can do, to bring back those who are still left amongst us.

The present Revival has restored a forgotten truth to us all,—*individual responsibility* and *the value of personal effort.*

"Go ye into all the world, and preach the Gospel to every creature," has been felt to be a personal command given to every Christian who loves his Lord.

"Go ye into the highways and hedges, and compel them to come in," has been obeyed by many who are not called to the ministry of the word and sacraments.

And God has blessed the lay-labourers; and men have been astonished at the wonderful results given in answer to prayer, combined with individual effort.

Oh! why should we not yet go a step further?

We want more oneness, more combined effort; less sectarian coldness, where our Lord has given His blessing richly; more sympathy and mutual dependence.

Is there not *one* bond of union for us all? *one* rallying Head, our common Lord Jesus Christ? And *one* Holy Spirit ready and willing to bless us all, and bring us together into sweet fellowship in Him?

In Christ, no individual believer, however humble or weak, can be powerless.

What God has enabled some, weak and helpless in themselves to effect, He can enable others also to do. But what might not be effected, if the Church of Christ realized her position and standing—*her oneness in Him!*

Oh, let us be shamed out of our selfishness and cold-heartedness, and earnestly send up our fervent prayer that we may one and all, "grow up into Him in all things, which is the head, even Christ; from whom the whole body fitly joined together and compacted by that which every joint supplieth, according to the effectual working in the measure of every part, maketh increase of the body unto the edifying of itself in love."

There *is* a work to be done.

Whilst men have slumbered and slept, Satan has been busy. He has taken an advantage of us. He has cast up a mighty barrier—a tremendous obstacle—to all religious and social advance. We appeal to magistrates, clergy, and philanthropists, what is it that thwarts, defeats, and nullifies all Christian efforts and schemes for the elevation and improvement of our working classes?

Is it not "*the drink?*"

What a cause for thankfulness that it is an external hindrance, which we can take up in our hands

and put out of the way! Let us take courage, and bless God that we *can* remove this great obstacle.

Though it be to ourselves personally no hindrance or snare, it is enough that it is THE *great obstacle* in the path of our brother.

Which of us, *as* CHRISTIANS, will act the part of the Priest and the Levite? Can we, *dare* we look on at our weak brother, who has stumbled, and pass by on the other side?

Shall our liberty continue to be a stumbling-block to them that are weak?

Through our knowledge shall any weak brother perish for whom Christ died?

Shall we not rather say, "All things are lawful for me, but all things are not expedient?

"Wherefore, if meat make my brother to offend, I will eat no meat while the world standeth, lest I make my brother to offend.

"It is good neither to eat flesh, nor to drink wine, nor anything whereby thy brother stumbleth, or is offended, or is made weak."

May God give us grace to serve Him faithfully in our day and generation *in this matter.* If the following pages shall in any way help or decide Christians to sympathise with the working classes in their war with "*the drink*," they will not be written in vain, and the blessing of many thousands who were ready to perish shall be theirs.

A Sad Retrospect.

"It never was in your soul
To play so ill a part,
But evil is wrought by want of thought,
As well as want of heart."

CHAPTER II.

SINCE the publication of "Haste to the Rescue" I have been constantly asked by persons at a distance, "Do tell us how you *began* your work amongst the people."

Now, it seems almost necessary first to go back a step and enter into some of my antecedents.

One sample of the past in Butcher Row will suffice when that street was my district.

In May 1851, a woman sent for me to visit her husband, who was on his death-bed. I shall call him Norfolk. He was a lead-worker, and, together with his wife and several lodgers, resided in one of the largest houses. Mrs. Norfolk, if she had been clean, would have made a most stately old lady. She was very erect, and had a profusion of white hair, but it was so tangled and disordered, it was difficult to believe that a comb had touched it for years. I had long ago visited her niece, Mrs. ——, in the same house during a long illness which terminated in her death. I knew, therefore, some of the scenes which I should have to witness. For instance, Mrs. Norfolk still kept poultry in her house. The staircase was wide and good, but perfectly dark when the bedroom

doors were shut. The fowls used to perch all day on the banisters in a sort of dose. Of course my visits were to them an unpardonable intrusion, and not unfrequently half-a-dozen of these creatures would fly off their perch with a disturbed cry, enough to rouse the house; and, shaking their soiled feathers in my face, would fill the air with dust and a most disagreeable smell. They would stalk into the sick chamber after me, glad to get into something like the light of heaven which streamed through the murky windows; and they would strain their necks to look at the invalid in the bed; and when I began to read or pray, the old cock would give a shrill crow with all his might, resolved to show himself master there.

Poor old Norfolk was thankful for my visits, yet I never could get at his heart. He heard all I had to say, but was evidently an uninterested listener. He acknowledged that he had never gone to any place of worship since his marriage, some forty years ago; but he felt quite satisfied that he did the same as others did, and he had "done no harm to any body," he felt "very comfortable" in his mind, &c. In short, nothing could be more unsatisfactory than his state was. He assured me that he felt so wearied with his work by Saturday nights that he always found it necessary to stay in bed on Sundays. Of course I believed him, and remember thinking "How can people expect working men to go to church on Sundays.

Only those who love Christ will ever make an effort to do so."

It never occurred to me that God would not give a law which it was impossible for the bulk of mankind to keep. The real causes of the Sunday incapacity and weariness were then utterly unknown to me.

I remember one *Saturday* evening, June 21st, 1851, feeling very unhappy. I had not seen Norfolk for two days. The weather was intensely hot, and I felt weak and ill, and altogether unequal to encounter the disagreeables which I knew awaited me in visiting him. The clock had struck eight. I said to my husband, "Dear Charles, I must go and see Norfolk to-night. I know it is late, but really I feel I have neglected him sadly; the fact is, I do not see much use in my visits to him. I am discouraged every time I go to him."

I went, and never shall I forget the scene. I went up the dark stairs unmolested; the bedroom door was open, but in vain did I knock, or ask for admittance. The noise within was quite terrible,—it was that of drunken mirth. At last, I gently went in; the scene defies description. The room was in thorough disorder; the sick man, as he sat up in his bed, held a glass of brandy and water in his uplifted hand, flourishing it in high style—he was shouting—his wife was very merry. An old man, a lodger, was the first to see me; he was half tipsy, indeed the whole party were so. I suppose my presence suggested my errand, for in one moment he dropped down on his knees, and reverently put his two hands together, as if in prayer.

Norfolk and his wife, becoming aware of my unwelcome presence, were silent in an instant, and the woman, bringing me a Bible, began to make preparations for my reading. I felt too sick at heart to stop, saying a few words about their present condition, I left them to their own reflections.

A few days more, and poor Norfolk died—no comment is necessary.

That Saturday night might have revealed a secret to me, but I thought it was a solitary case.

And yet for many years we used to be awoke out of our first sleep, nearly every Saturday night, by the sounds of drunken mirth and revelry; and I remember we always noticed that women's voices were conspicuous in the uproar. It must be mentioned that within two minutes' walk from our house there are eleven public or beer houses, all in our parish.

In looking back to those times, a number of facts and incidents crowd my memory. I feel overwhelmed with astonishment, combined with shame and sorrow, that it never occurred to us to lay the axe to the root of the evil—in other words, *to wage war with the* DRINK.

The words of our blessed Lord sound in my ears,

He which spoke against Chorazin and Bethsaida: "If the mighty works which were done in you had been done in Tyre and Sidon, they would have repented long ago in sackcloth and ashes." And the anguish caused by the recollection of past opportunities of usefulness, lost, for ever, more from want of *knowledge of facts* than from wilful neglect,—all this at times almost sinks me into despair, except for other words of our gracious Lord, "All that the Father giveth me shall come to me," which reassure and comfort me. He will take care that His own shall not be lost.

On June 29th, 1851, I wrote in my Sunday journal:—"Second Sunday after Trinity. I have just heard of Norfolk's death, in my Butcher Row district.

"O Lord, humble me in my own sight, for my negligence of this man.

"Deliver me from bloodguiltiness. Have mercy upon me.

"Surely if Christ were not at Thy right hand to plead for me, I must perish for ever.

"Oh, give me a double portion of Thy Holy Spirit, for my need is great. I am utterly sinful and vile.

"I never felt a hotter day. Dulness marked my services at Church and at home.

"Did my Saviour think of the heat when He went about the towns and villages, beneath the burning sun of an Eastern clime?

"Did He not say, when He sat, wearied with His journey, on Jacob's well, so wearied and faint that He he asked for a cup of cold water from the Samaritan woman, 'My meat is to do the will of Him that sent Me?'

"Lord Jesus, at Thy table I asked Thee to-day to make me like Thyself—Thou canst do all things. Oh, have mercy upon me. Give me fervent love to Thee, that I may deny myself, take up my cross, and follow Thee.

"Lord Jesus, answer the prayer which I prayed before Thee at the house of that poor widow in Butcher Row. She is still left. Open her heart to seek Thee, lead her, forsake her not. *Amen.*"

Light breaks in.

"There ariseth light in the darkness."

CHAPTER III.

The question with which my last chapter commenced still remains to be answered.

But we must first go back to one more scene. An extract from a letter to the author of "English Hearts and English Hands" will best recall it; it is published in "Haste to the Rescue."

"Last winter, November 1856, a young butcher, our parishioner, named Bromley, was killed by a man, more or less under the influence of drink, in a crowd that had been collected in the Market Square by the playing of a band of music at the unseasonable hour of eleven at night. This event caused a great sensation amongst the people. It is too long a story to tell now. After the funeral my husband gave a solemn address in the churchyard, as he noticed here were a large number of butchers' men present whom he had never seen in church before. The opportunity was too precious to be lost. He told them, in conclusion, there should be a special service for them at three o'clock on the following Sunday afternoon.

"They seemed much impressed by his address;

and to our great comfort, between two and three hundred persons, *chiefly men*, attended that service on the following Sunday. They were placed in pews. There was hardly one of those rough, strange-looking men who did not weep during the fervent appeal made to them. We sang,

"'There is a fountain filled with blood.'

I saw many sit down with their faces buried in their handkerchiefs. I was so affected I could not sound a note. To our great disappointment there were not ten of these men who ever came again to church, although notice was given that the service should be continued at that same hour every Sunday.

"I see now if we had followed up the people . . . but it is no use to make vain regrets. The men are still here; I believe they are all living. It is evident they have not blunted every feeling. They have yet a soft place in their hearts. I forgot to say, when that first special service took place, my husband asked all those who wished to become members of a reading-room and night-school to give their names to him in the vestry. Twenty-five men came forward, and the night-school was started immediately; but it, also, proved a failure. I believe only two or three of these men attended. The rest who came were young lads from all parts of the town, chiefly from other parishes, whose object seemed to be diversion, rather than improvement; so the night-school was given up."

One Sunday afternoon I went to every house in Butcher Row, to ascertain how many persons went to any place of worship; and amongst forty-three *families* I found to my dismay that about six individuals alone, chiefly women, attended Divine Service once or twice on Sundays. The rest went nowhere.

Only the women were to be seen, as the men were lying down upstairs, or else drinking in public-houses. I pleaded with tears at every house, many were affected and promised amendment. Mrs. Norfolk actually came to church on the following Sunday, clean and neat. Alas! it was but a short-lived change, for she never came again, and some months afterwards she had a fit, from the effects of which she never recovered her speech or consciousness: and she died after a few days' illness.

Another woman, who was known to be a drunkard, was on another Sunday most earnestly pleaded with. I implored her to come that same evening to church. She was affected to tears; promised to come *next* Sunday. In vain it was urged, 'Next Sunday you may be in eternity, oh, come now, I beseech you, come, Jesus will receive you.' That day week she died of apoplexy.

Such was the state of things in our parish up to the close of 1857.

There was a large number of precious souls wholly inaccessible to any good influence. The thought often weighed on our minds. But it was not till we read that wonderful book "English Hearts and English Hands." in January, 1858, that we saw how the case could be met. I never shall forget the thrilling interest with which we read of the Sunday cottage-readings, and the night-visiting. The possibility of my carrying on such had never entered my head. *It lighted up a new idea.* I resolved, in the might of Jesus, to begin at once a loving, earnest work amongst our home heathen,—to make a business of it—to give myself wholly to the Lord for the rest of my life, if He would only deign to use me—for winning souls for Christ and glory—men, women, and children. Why should the *men* be systematically neglected as they hitherto have been everywhere? What clergyman hardly knows the faces of the *working men* in his parish?

On January 4th, 1858, my husband received a summons to attend the funeral of a dear friend in a distant county. On his return home, he met with a slight accident at one of the railway stations, which he considered too trivial to notice, but which eventually laid him aside for six weeks.

During that time he begged me to visit the poor in the half of the parish which fell to his share for that month. Butcher Row and the surrounding streets were included in that division. There were several sick persons on their death-beds, to whom I had to go daily for him.

God's blessing was earnestly sought, and given. My heart was stirred up to go from house to house amongst those in health, especially amongst the butchers' men, for I had never forgotten the scene in church in November 1856.

Robert Wilding, our sexton, a butcher, sixty-nine years of age, lay on his death-bed in one of the passages in Butcher Row. Poor fellow! he had been all his life a hard drinker; during the first four months of his illness he was not visited, for we did not know he was ill.* God overruled this for his good, for he said to his daughter, "Mr. Wightman and Mr. L—— have forgotten me; *I must pray for myself.*" Thus he was not suffered to rest the responsibility of his soul on the parson, as too many people do, but came himself to the throne of grace, in much ignorance doubtless, but nevertheless heartily. When I first visited him there was not that conviction of sin which one desired to see; but as the Holy Spirit opened up his mind and heart to receive the truth as it is in Jesus, he felt greatly distressed for the life he had led,

* It is very trying to a pastor when people do not send to let him know that they are ill, but this is often the case from carelessness and unconcern.

and was most earnest in his pleading for mercy through Christ. As I sat beside him he would pray, as if unconscious of my presence, "Blessed Jesus, blessed Jesus, have mercy on me a sinner." That sweet hymn, "I lay my sins on Jesus," was a great comfort to him. His mind was perfectly clear to the last. I saw him shortly before his death; a quarter of an hour before he died he asked for me; his last words were spoken in a strong voice, "Jesus, my God, my God, help me."

A week before dear Robert Wilding's death, he told me that he could not sleep at nights, the men in that passage were so terribly drunken and noisy, it was quite awful to hear them; he added, "I have been quite as bad as they." On coming out of his house that day a woman who lived opposite waylaid me, earnestly entreating me to get her husband to sign the pledge, "Please don't ever let him know as I asked you."

I was sorely puzzled at this request, not knowing how to set about it. However, I promised to do my best, thinking it could do no harm to try. But I disliked the pledge altogether then. After calling several times during the week, and never finding Hawkins in, at last I was successful on the following Sunday. He was alone in the house upstairs, having gone to lie down. On hearing a knock at the door, he came down, leading a little child by the hand.

Being a perfect stranger to him, I felt embarrassed, and not knowing how to begin my errand, I said in a beseeching voice, without any preface, "O Mr. Hawkins, will you sign the pledge?"

I shall never forget how thankfully he accepted my offer. He looked so very grateful, and confessed that drink made him mad and brutal. Fearing that he attributed too much power to the pledge, I added, "There is no strength given in signing, my friend; the pledge is not Christ; you must get strength from *Him* to keep you from temptation."

"Yes, but I shall have an answer to give when they want me to drink, if I sign it."

I sent the Registrar of the Shrewsbury Total Abstinence Society next day to receive Hawkins's signature. He told me afterwards, "I never saw a man sign so heartily in my life." He signed January 18th, 1858, for a twelvemonth, and kept it, and though he did break after that, thank God he soon after returned.

Next day in visiting Sarah Stedman, who was dying of consumption, to my astonishment she received me with fits of laughter. I could not make it out. At last, as soon as she had recovered her voice, she said, "So —— —— has signed the pledge! that rackety man! O ma'am, do try and get my husband! It would be such a thing if he could be got to do the same. I could die happy then."

"But he is become such a quiet, steady man, Sarah."

"O ma'am, you don't know anything about it! The *temptations* he 've got, AND THE COMPANIONS! Oh, if you could but get Dick, he'd keep it for you, for he'd do anything in the world for you, because you 've been so good to me."

I promised her, seeing that nothing else would satisfy her mind, but I disliked the pledge then. "Tell him that I wish to speak to him at three o'clock this afternoon."

He came. I shall never forget that hour in our dining-room—the most solemn I ever spent. I felt that eternal issues were at stake. It was the turning-point in his life. I saw the hard struggle *to give up all,* for I knew not till then, that with the working man signing the pledge involves nearly every thing included in "the world, the flesh, and the devil." At last he sobbed as if his heart would break; and then, humble and gentle as a little child, he rose up, and said, "I'll come to-morrow night at eight o'clock, and I'll keep it too."

"I believe you, Richard."

"And I'll bring six more to sign, as soon as I can get them."

True to his word, he came next day, January 20th, 1858, and signed. At this time he was working for the Great Western Railway Company, loading and unloading wagons at their office on the Welsh Bridge. He was also employed at the porter-stores, taking heavy casks on a truck to village public-houses all round the neighbourhood.

Amidst such temptations the leaving off drink was soon known by all his companions. Many a jeer and taunt was received, but he held on firmly—good-humouredly bearing all, and winning as many as he could to the cause of temperance.

One day I met him taking a heavy load on a truck. His bright look of pleasure spoke volumes of hearty welcome; not wishing to hinder him, I walked by his side as far as we had to go the same way, talking to him. A man passed us, calling out in a sneering whisper, "Teetotal!" Stedman's countenance grew brighter as he quietly nodded to the man, taking no further notice of him except to say, "Poor fellow! it would be a good job, ma'am, if he'd follow my example, and turn teetotal also!"

Does any one feel disposed to find fault with a lady thus subjecting herself to an unpleasant moment, by walking beside a working man engaged as Stedman was? It is an honour to stand by and strengthen a brother or sister by our countenance and sympathy, in public or in private,—an honour I love.

It is to be regretted that no notes were taken of dear Sarah Stedman's illness. An extract from a letter written at that time to my sister is nearly the only record left:—

"I saw Stedman's wife again last evening, after church. She again gave me a fervent blessing, as I knelt beside her, repeating texts of Scripture and scraps of hymns.

"'Oh, I shall bless you through eternity; you first put me in the way!'

"'No, do not bless me: bless and praise Jesus Christ; He died for you. I am but a poor sinner like yourself, only an instrument in His hands.'

"'But *you did* first put me in the way, and I shall bless you, and rejoice with you at His right hand for ever. I was contented with myself; and you told me to pray for the Holy Spirit to show me what a sinner I was; and I did pray, and He showed me Jesus, and *then* I knew what a vile sinner I had been—how I had gone regular to church, but never prayed or taken heed to sermons. Oh, I might as well never have gone, for the good it did me; but He has washed all my sins away in His blood!' She added, after pausing to rest, 'I shall so welcome you when you come to heaven!'"

On Sunday, January 24th, I began a cottage reading between our Services, at three o'clock P.M, and arranged to meet the people again at eight o'clock on Tuesday nights for the same purpose.

For the comfort and encouragement of any ladies who would wish to follow the same plan, I would say that it was not half so formidable as it appeared in anticipation. No one could have felt more nervous than I did, especially when my husband charged me to begin with a hymn. The solemnity of gathering together those who never attend any place of worship, and of being the first to speak to them of Jesus, took away every lesser thought; indeed, *self* could not intrude in such a scene. I found the most thorough attention and decorum. Many a time nearly all were in tears. We began our first meeting with six persons, two of whom were children; and gradually our numbers increased, until no private room would hold us. In the summer we met in our garden, and subsequently we removed to St. Alkmond's school-room, a place which has become very dear to us all, as the birthplace of many who shall be our crown of glory and our rejoicing in the day of our Lord's appearing.

We soon found that the men who did not sign the pledge gradually left our meetings, and went back altogether to their old haunts and companions. But those who signed continued amongst us, and never thought of absenting themselves from the meetings; and, in a very short time, each member appeared at church also, which was most satisfactory to me.

From that time to the present the meetings have been regularly carried on.

Our plan is very simple. We begin with a hymn, in which all join most heartily; then prayer; after that, a portion of Scripture, with an exposition and application, as hearty, affectionate, and to the point, as it can be made. On Tuesday nights, after the Scripture exposition, some extract from any book illustrating the Bible subject is occasionally read; in the earlier days of my work, "Hearts and Hands" was listened to with thrilling interest; since then we have given sketches from the lives of holy men, such as Havelock, Hedley Vicars, &c. If any event has occurred of public or local interest, it is always taken as a theme, and a full and simple narrative given in our own words, which is better than reading it. For instance, the account of the marriage of the Princess Royal, and the glimpse it gave us of the homely hearts, full of love and affection, in the royal family, made a charming theme for Tuesday night, Feb. 7th, 1858, when those who were present will remember the pleasure with which they received copies of the "Illustrated London News," containing pictures of the whole ceremony, and a portrait of our beloved Princess. These portraits were framed and hung up in their cottages afterwards, and are highly prized. The eclipse of the sun, which took place a few weeks after, gave a delightful opportunity of explaining, in the simplest manner possible, the mystery in which all that concerns the heavenly bodies is wrapped to the uneducated mind. The little children who were present had the pleasure afterwards of eating the oranges which were used in illustrating our first astronomical lecture!

We always close our meetings with a hymn and prayer.

We have never altered the religious character of our meetings, nor omitted the Scripture-reading and exposition. To this I attribute the rich blessing God has given us. The people have come, wearied and worn with their daily struggles, and their daily toil; their hearts grieved with the unfeeling taunts or thoughtless jeers of fellow-workmen or old companions, and feeling keenly the want of sympathy from those who ought to have accounted it an honour to stand by them. Thus, words about the Great Redeemer, spoken in love *by one who sympathised with them,* have found entrance into hearts unused to hallowed thoughts; and many have learned to love and to worship that Saviour of whom they would probably never have heard if they had not signed the pledge.

A Band of Faithful Witnesses.

"In the mouth of two or three witnesses shall every word be established."

CHAPTER IV.

We were reading our letters quietly one morning after breakfast, in November 1859, when my husband handed me one of his, saying, with an arch smile, "Here, I leave *you* to answer this!"

I looked at it with no small curiosity, and found it was written by a stranger, the Rev. ——, Rector of ——. I read on till I came to the following sentence, "Tell your good wife, Almost thou persuadest me to be a teetotalist," when, laying down the letter, I exclaimed, "Oh! I do not like this. We must have no '*almost*' in the matter. I will write to him by to-day's post."

"Now take my advice, Julia," said my sage cousin, Penelope W——, who was staying with us; "take my advice, and do nothing rashly, or you will damage your cause."

"You are quite right, dear. I know what I will do. I will tell the people all about it to-night at our meeting, and ask some of them to write for me their own simple testimony to the good teetotalism has done them. Of course, if Mr. —— has read *the facts* in connexion with our work here, and is only 'almost persuaded' about the benefits of total abstinence, nothing that I can say will change his views, or shake his prejudices! So the people shall try what *they* can do, for it is *most important* to gain a *clergyman* to our cause."

"But pray finish reading the letter you have laid down in your indignation; there are some special objections to be answered."

I took up the letter again, and read something about "teetotalism being unscriptural," &c., questions which the writer wished me to solve.

"Very well. He shall have *facts* instead of arguments."

That night, after our meeting, I laid the case before the people, and asked them to write letters, addressed either to myself, or to Mr. ——, and to let me have them by Thursday evening.

Great interest was excited, together with no small amusement, by this unexpected little event.

On the day appointed twelve letters were brought to me. As three of them have already appeared in print, I will here add some of the others, which are equally worthy of being preserved. I kept a literal copy of the letters, sending the originals to Mr. ——.

Suffice it to say, these letters were read by our good friend, and brought a most hearty and satisfactory response from him, in which he gave in his adhesion to the total abstinence cause, assuring us that he could not withstand such a band of faithful witnesses in its favour.

No. 1. From a labourer, who served for sixteen years in the 53d Regiment, he signed the pledge, Nov. 2d, 1858:—

DEAR REV. SIR,—I am one that has been checked in my downward course by the medium of total abstinence. My dear and very worthy Christian advocate, Mrs. W——, has been the means in God's hands of turning not only myself, but scores in this town, from that awful sin of drunkenness, which was ruining our souls and bodies, and bringing our families to beggary and want.

Thanks be to God, not only this, but through her instrumentality many of us have been brought to see our sinful state as sinners before God, and made to cry out for pardon and forgiveness through the blood of a crucified Saviour. And we trust that, through the grace of God, we shall be enabled to go on our way rejoicing.

I for one feel that I am a poor, ignorant, unworthy creature, and trust alone to the merits of my Saviour for salvation and forgiveness.

I shall be glad to see more souls added to our number daily, and would to God that the ministers of

the Church would set the example and advocate the cause in every place!

Our dear minister, Mr. Young, has kindly lent us the vestry-room,* and we meet at seven A.M. every Sunday for prayer, and we find it good to meet together to seek the grace of God, to help us on for the future.

May the Lord prosper the good lady who took up the cause, and may she long live to go forth in the good work.

From your humble servant,

No. 2. From a man who works at nights every alternate week, he signed on March 27th, 1859:—

Rev. Sir,—In consequence of a letter received by our much-respected benefactress, Mrs. W——, I have taken up my pen to give you my opinion of total abstinence in connexion with Christianity.

I signed the pledge on the 27th of March; and I regret to say that for several years previous to that time, I lived in total neglect of public worship and private devotion, and often neglected my work at the risk of being dismissed from it, and cared little for my home, and dissipated my health, and strength, and youth. But I thank God for the change wrought in me since I signed the pledge, although I have been subject to

* This meeting now takes place in St. Alkmond's Schoolroom, and about sixty persons attend.

great temptation among my fellow-workmen; but by the grace of God, and the religious instructions, consolations, and admonitions, which I have received from our much-respected friend Mrs. W—— (for whom I shall ever pray), I have been able to resist temptation, and to attend the means of grace; which I am prepared to say that no man addicted to drinking can do with any benefit to his soul while his brain is in a state of confusion, and his body in a state of disorder, from the effects of the spirit which he has imbibed; and therefore I am convinced there can never be Christianity joined with intemperance, for it is the interest of the publican to keep men from serving God; for when a working man becomes a Christian, he must be abstemious as Jonadab, the son of Rechab; see the Apostle Paul to the Romans, xiii. 13, and 1 Cor. x. 21, and many other passages.

In conclusion, I beg to say that I think if every clergyman's wife in England would follow the example of the indefatigable disinterestedness of Mrs. W——, the prisons would be empty, and the churches would be filled.

And that it may soon be the case, is the sincere and earnest prayer of your humble servant,

———

No. 3. From a stone-mason, he signed the pledge June 21st, 1859:—

Dear Sir,—At our dear President's request I have

made bold to address a few lines to you, hoping it will strengthen the cause of total abstinence with you and with your parishioners.

In the first place, I thank God, which in His goodness and mercy put it into my head to join St. Alkmond's Total Abstinence Society. For these reasons:—I am a stone-mason, and I am very sorry to say most of our craft are fond of intoxicating drinks.

When I was drinking, as soon as I got my money on the Saturday evening, I got a pint as soon as I could before I went home.

As soon as I had had my tea, off to the public-house, staying there till they turned me out. I would then be quite drunk.

Sunday morning come, no thought of church, but some more drink as soon as I could to enliven me from the previous evening, for my head was racked with pain. I then had no thought for the future in my mad career.

I left my wife alone while I caroused at the public-house, and my neglect was her ruin. She formed an intimacy with another man, my lodger, and eloped with him, robbing me of everything, getting me in debt to the extent of 14*l.*; and I alone am to blame, for I neglected my home for the public-house. I then saw what I had done, ruined myself and her likewise. And I said, "This drink has done with me, as it has done with thousands, ruined my character and hopes."

I then said, With God's help I will never drink intoxicating drink any more; and by God's mercy I have not yet done so. I can now do my work better, in less time. I have more time on a Saturday, and I enjoy better health than I have for years past. But better than all, since I have been a total abstainer, I can look to my Maker more. I see that I have a soul to save, that I never troubled with before when I was drinking. I had been married five years and eight months when I turned total abstainer. During that time I never went to church or chapel, but four times,—to my shame be it said.

But, thanks to total abstinence and kind instructions of our most worthy President,—God bless her!—I now attend a place of worship twice every Sunday, our own lectures in the week, and other lectures and prayer-meetings in the week. I have shaken off my old companions, and, with God's help, I will be a better man to God and society.

I must now conclude, with my kind love to you, and may God's blessing be with you, and your parishioners, and strengthen them in the cause of total abstinence.

I remain your humble servant,

No. 4. From a nailor, who signed in March 1858:

These are a few facts of my own experience. In 1858, Mrs. W——, our kind president and founder of our happy society, came to our house to see my wife, as she had lately been confined.

It was in the month of March. I came in at the same time she was there, and she told me she had begun a total abstinence society, and asked me if I would sign the pledge and become a member. I hesitated a little, and this kind lady gave me about three days to consider on it. Accordingly I did make up my mind I would sign, and become a member of this lady's society. And it has proved to be the best day's work I ever did in my life, and daily do I return thanks to the Lord for sending and stirring up the heart of that Christian lady our President, who is working amongst us daily and hourly.

I then began to go to the cottage-reading on Tuesday nights for some time, it was then held at Charles Wilding's. There was but few members then, and they were such happy meetings.

I cannot express myself how happy I felt—quite a different life to what I had been leading. I kept firm to my pledge about sixteen weeks. One day I was rather upset in my mind, and at the same time I met with some of my old companions, went to a public-house, broke my pledge to drown my grief, which made it ten times worse. I did not go to the meeting that night. As I had never missed before, our kind President came to our house the next day to know if I was well, as I did not attend the meeting. My wife told the President that I had broken the pledge last night.

She asked what time I should be in, and my wife could not tell the lady. The next day there was sent to our house a letter from our kind President for me, and a very kind and encouraging letter it was to have from a lady. It was to ask me to come back and join her "brave and happy little band" again; and oh, how glad I was of such a letter, and how many times did I read it!

After this I made up my mind, *with the help of God,* never to taste no more. I signed the pledge with our kind President again the next day, June 27th, 1858, and I never have since tasted drink.

I attend Divine service twice every Sunday since I have been a total abstainer from those poisons, which are the curse of our country.

At our meetings, which are on Sunday nights, after evening service, and on Tuesday nights, there attends from 150 to upwards of 200 persons, all looking respectable and well. The chief of these men, and myself for one, used to be too fond of that cursed poison.

I was fifteen years, and was never in a place of worship above six times. And what was the reason why? I was a drunkard, and had got no clothes to go in, and was disrespected by everybody. What a happy change! Blessed be His holy Name for it!

Since I have been a teetotaller, I have expended on myself and family, furniture, and shop-tools, the sum of 17*l.* that the publicans used to have, beside the extra comforts I have in my own house, as I used to deprive myself and family on.

So now I must conclude, returning the Lord thanks for this happy change, and for sending such a kind Christian lady as our President among us poor working men.

I remain your humble servant,

No. 5. From a labourer, who signed Dec. 21st, 1858:—

Rev. Sir,—It is with a deep sense of my unworthiness, that I now address these few lines to you, on behalf of St. Alkmond's Total Abstinence Society, of which I feel to thank God that ever He inclined my heart to turn in to hear the instructions taught by its worthy President, who is the sole author and founder of this great and mighty work.

Nothing short of the power of the great God could have supported her to accomplish so great a work. It is better than fifteen months since I joined its ranks, and it is the greatest blessing, through God's mercy, that I ever enjoyed.

For thirty years have I revelled in drunkenness. Who can picture the life of a drunkard? his home brought to desolation; conscience hurting him; and he never at rest but when revelling with companions reckless as himself.

But I will not dwell on this time of misery, but turn to the bright side of the question.

Reverend Sir, *persuade* a man to leave off drinking, *then* he will *begin to think that all is not right with him; that something must be done.* He begins to feel that he has a soul to be saved,—a soul that must live for ever in happiness or in misery. Well; is it not worth *any effort* to try to save that soul? Oh, yes! oh, yes! And, instead of going in search of intoxicating drinks, as he was wont to do in former times, he turns in with the people of God into His house of prayer, there crying, in the fulness of his soul, "What must I do to be saved?" May this be the cry of every drunkard!

Oh, what a blessed privilege do we enjoy, that, after a Sabbath spent in the house of God, we have another privilege! Fancy yourself in our school-room, where upwards of 200 of us may assemble, eagerly devouring the holy instructions which drop from the lips of our worthy President.

Oh, what a happy change! Would that all ministers would put their shoulder to the wheel! If they would consider well the command of the Lord to Aaron, in Lev. x. 8, 9, 10, and following verses. We find total abstinence is an act sanctioned by God. Throughout the whole tenor of Scripture, what awful warnings there are against drunkenness, especially in the book of Habakkuk, chap. ii. verses 15, 16.

Oh, that men would be wise, and serve the Lord in time, with no vain-glorious boasting, but with meekness and sincerity of spirit!

Sir, I must bring my epistle to a close, hoping that you do excuse anything that you may see amiss in it, as I am a labourer, and not one accustomed to write, the occupation I follow keeps me out of practice.

I remain, Reverend Sir,

Yours sincerely,

No. 6. Indited by a sawyer, and taken down by me in his presence, he signed Dec. 7th, 1858:—

During the last thirteen months before I signed the pledge, I ran up, as trust-money, an account, for 1*l.* 11*s.* 9*d.* at the —— public-house, besides spending from four to ten shillings a-week, which I paid for drink at various other houses. We used to drink, play cards and dominoes.

I nearly broke my wife's heart at last.

She had just had her twelfth child. All the twelve lived with us together. My eldest daughter was twenty-one years old. When the baby was nearly two months old, I was at the railway station, watching the trains coming in, to keep me from the public-house (I sometimes stayed there three or four hours of a night, for want of a place to sit quiet in, to get off going to the public). I felt unhappy and uneasy in my mind. I knowed nothing about your Society then, or I'd have gladly come and joined. That night, it was a Monday, John Simmons came into the Station, and said to me, "Why don't you sign the pledge as I have done?" He had been about two months, and spoke well of it and of you. I signed December 7th, 1858, but I found no comfort to my heart, though I attended church regular for twenty-two Sundays, and your meetings also. I never felt myself a sinner then,—not until I broke the pledge on April 5, 1859.

It was then I felt miserable; and I saw what misery I brought on *you*,—how terrible *you* took it to heart; *that* cut me up most of all.

I joined again soon, the next day after. And one day in April or May, I can't tell which, I heard Mr. Wightman tell in church about the prodigal son; and it came all over me, to think there was mercy for such as me. And I thought of what my mother said to me before she died, all about that very chapter, and I forgot I was there in church, and I cried like a child. I shall never forget it the longest day I live.

I then began to pray to the Lord to help me to keep the pledge this time faithful. I prayed night and day—I prayed day and night, *earnest!* I prayed at my work at the sawpit, and as I walked in the streets, and as I sat at home, that He would forgive me my sins, and change my heart. And I remembered how cross I was to my wife the first weeks when I signed in December. And I prayed to the Lord to help me to keep my temper, for I am very quick and passionate. And now we have such peace in our home. I have cause to speak up for the teetotal pledge. With me it was *the first step to God* (after I broke it, I mean). If I had never signed the pledge, I should never have come to your meetings; and then I should never have come to church. Your meetings brought me to church.

And now, I come every month to the Lord's table—and I feel the Lord has heard my prayer, and he has accepted me through my Saviour, and washed me from all my sins.

When I read this through to ——, with tears in his eyes he said, "Yes—you've just wrote what I wanted; only I wish now as how I'd got some one else to have wrote it out, instead of *you*, to have told what I feel towards you and the master for all you have done for me, but I couldn't have asked *you* to write *that*, could I?"

Dear honest man! what it will be to meet him and his fellows in heaven!

I do not apologise for having retained the warm-hearted expressions about myself which occur in the preceding letters, I could not hurt the feelings of my grateful and affectionate brothers by omitting them.

No. 7. From one who never was drunken, a labourer; he signed July 26th, 1859:—

Sir,—I feel that I have cause to praise God that ever I signed the teetotal pledge. I feel the real comforts from sobriety in every way.

While listening to the preaching of the Gospel, my hard heart often got softened since I signed to become a total abstainer from all intoxicating drinks.

I have been to the Lord's table, and feel truly thankful that I was found worthy—I should still have been *almost a Christian* if I had not had a dear friend that encouraged me to sign.

In Deut. xxix. 19, 20, my Bible tells me that all the curses that are written in this book shall be upon the drunkard, and the Lord shall blot out his name from under heaven.

Yours respectfully,

George Raymond.

"The drama of life is now changèd again,
And I stand up the free man,—I've broken my chain!
Ye friends of the outcast, who snatched me from death,
In thanks for my rescue I now raise my breath.
O! I wish that my heart years since felt as now,
A long time ago! a long time ago!"

CHAPTER V.

It was a lovely spring morning, April 1860; the rain fell fast yet softly—it was impossible to grudge it, after the long cold dry season, though it interfered with one's comfort in the streets—it was so evidently wanted. And the hush of wind made it descend as if it had a special mission upon earth.

The limes in the Quarry sent forth a sweet fragrance as I passed; and here and there a garden lilac and early shrub filled the air with their welcome scent.

Twelve names were down in my list to visit that morning; but in passing dear old George Raymond's house, I thought, as the shower kept increasing, it would be nice to stop and have a chat with him and his wife.

They were delighted to see me.

"Well, my friend, I congratulate you; I sent you your *twelvemonths'* card last night!"

"But I wasn't at your meeting last night."

"No, I know you were not, so I sent it you by your district visitor. It was too late last night when we closed the meeting for him to bring it to you, but you will receive it from him to-day without fail."

"Thank you, ma'am, I shall be very proud to have it."

"And so shall I be, to see it hanging up in your house. Now, you promised me the other day, that when you had finished your twelvemonth, you would give me a few facts about your past life, for my new book; could you do so to-day?"

"My wife and me was talking about it yesterday. But we don't know where we are to begin."

"Were you ever at a Sunday-school?"

"No, I never was, for there was no such thing known when I was a child; but my father kept a school himself. It was the best school in the neighbourhood. He lived at W——. He failed when I was four years old, and then grandfather took me to live with him. He had a large farm, and kept a public-house at W——, and he reared me from the time I was four years old."

"Ah! you learned to drink there, I suppose?"

"Well, as for that, I was in the midst of it all my youth, but I don't know that I got into it there, for it was a very respectable house, they never would draw for any one after ten o'clock, and we closed at that time, let what would come."

"When did you first get too much drink?"

"Why I got tipsy at eight or nine years of age,

SHREWSBURY.

that was my first time, and I had cause to recollect it, for I got a good flogging for it; they were very strict with me."

He then told me that he was apprenticed at thirteen or fourteen years of age. "That was the place I got ruined at, for master drank terrible. I had to fetch him home at nights, and sometimes had to sit up all night with him too."

"When did you come to Shrewsbury?"

"In 1813; and I got work directly, I worked for the same master many years. I could work all day, and get drunk at nights, and so I carried on. Master could always depend upon catching me at home in a morning, for I used to stop in bed after drinking all night—and yet I was always ready for work if wanted."

"You must have had a good constitution, and outlived many a drinking companion."

"Yes, *there's not one of my old companions left; they are all dead through the drink.* They could not eat when they were getting drunk all the while—it's not one in a thousand who can—and so *they died for want of food*—but I could eat well all the time."

"When did you marry?"

"In 1822."

"What! have you two lived together nearly forty years?"

"Yes," said Mrs. Raymond, her eyes filling with tears; "nobody knows but God and myself what I've gone through. But the Lord kept up my heart. The trouble was sanctified to me."

"Oh, how merciful of God to make your bitter days a blessing to your soul! You shall have cause to bless and praise God for that to all eternity."

"Yes; for I didn't know Him nor love Him till sorrow drove me to the Throne of Grace. Many a night I've sat up for my husband till all the neighbours would be gone to bed, when he came home; but I never felt lonely, I found Jesus to be always present with me." Here the poor woman wept.

"It was a heavy disappointment about money that drove me to drink worse. My grandfather died, and my aunt kept on the farm and the public-house; and when she died, she left it all away from me to a nephew of her husband's. She had no children of her own, so she made a god of this lad, and she educated him for a lawyer, and settled him in London. And I got so disappointed at her not leaving me a farthing (for she had got rich by the farm and the public-house) that I fell to drinking desperately."

"And yet that was making bad matters worse."

"That's quite true, indeed."

"Did you ever go on tramp?"

"Oh, I've been to Birmingham; but I hadn't

much occasion for anything of that sort—I could get a pretty tidy living by *scheming* all the time; in short, I lived by scheming."

"What does that mean?"

"I could always get credit; I would get the money beforehand, they knew they was sure of it again. I would work for the shops, so I got into debt on speculation, and as they was sure I would pay them again, I was trusted. I've received sixty pounds at a time from the shops."

"And did you continue a drunken and scheming life all the time?"

"No, for I signed the pledge fifteen years ago, but my keeping the pledge then was very different to my keeping it now, for I was not as I am now; I used to drink ginger-beer and smoke my pipe in the public-houses then. *I never gave up my company then; how could I stand firm for long when that was the case?*" He begged me to make a strong point of this for the sake of other persons.

"Did you never get into difficulties?"

"Yes, indeed, and sold many a good piece of furniture, and not at their true value either. But I never was so bad off, but my wife always had something to eat, she was never starved through me. I had a good business, and with good management I might have kept five men to work; but I was always spending my money before I received it, and then I would work all the harder to make it up, and then go scheming again. But with all my drinking I never got into trouble like some; I was never fined, and never brought up before the magistrates."

"Well, how was it you thought of coming to me?"

"I don't know how it was, except it was God sent me. I shall always pray for you every day, for you have been the means of saving me. If I had gone on drinking at the rate I was doing six months before I signed, I should not have been alive now."

"From Christmas till May he drank incessant," added his wife.

"Yes, I was six months at it, *constantly tipsy*, and *let no one say after that, that it hurts a man to leave it off suddenly.* I left it off at one stroke *at sixty-eight years of age, after forty years' drunkenness*, and I've felt all the better for it in health. But I am getting old now, so I must not wonder if I shouldn't continue to feel so strong as I am. I shall never believe it's through teetotalism hurting me if I don't, for I feel ten years younger now than I did when I signed."

"I've cause to bless you and pray for you, for saving my husband, but it's the Gospel only, after all, that can save his soul, and I pray it may be blessed to him yet."

"O Raymond, you know my only desire in getting any one to sign the pledge is to bring them to Christ. Do come to Him with your whole heart, for *the time is short*, and *you* have none to lose. Do think of God's mercy to you. *I want to meet you in Heaven.*"

"I know you do; and I am sure all your desire in getting us to give up the drink is that we may *cling to Christ* and be saved. I shall always pray for you, for having brought me out of drunkenness."

"But I do not feel that I deserve any credit. I never came and sought you out. You came to me a perfect stranger."

"True, but if you had not had a society, and if we hadn't heard of you as *a friend who cared for us*, we should none of us have come to you. So it all comes to the same thing, and we shall know you in Heaven as our friend."

"I think, Raymond, we shall then see so much more than we do now the hand of God in all that has concerned our lives here, His love in drawing us to Him, and arranging all our circumstances, that we shall not think so much of our fellow-sinners who influenced us to come to Jesus, as we shall of His grace, mercy, and love."

"That's true, but we must always feel a special bond of union towards those who were the instruments in God's hands of bringing us to Him."

"Well, it will be so, I suppose, for I know I shall feel a special tie to each one who is in my society."

"Of course you will, ma'am, like what a minister feels."

"Say rather like what a *mother* feels, though some of my children are somewhat older than I am!" smiling at dear old Raymond as I spoke, who could not help smiling too; and he added,—

"I shall never forget the day I came to you. As I passed Mr. Cooke the dyer, I had a great struggle in myself whether I should come or no. I leaned against the railings of St. Alkmond's churchyard, the devil was busy tempting me. I half resolved to go back. I am certain if I had not signed that day, I should not have been alive by next morning. I was tempted to do something desperate. I was mad with myself for having gone on so terribly with the drink, and for ruining my missus."

He could scarcely get on for tears,—

"*Thank God*, she has had *one* happy year—*one* year's comfort and quietness," he added.

"Oh! *how thankful* I am you came to me."

"Yes, God brought me to myself, and I made a resolution that I would come up and face you manfully to sign the pledge. Oh! if ministers of religion only knew what power they lose by keeping aloof from the total abstinence cause, and what influence the pledge has in bringing many a poor sinner out of drunkenness to Christ, who through the drink is kept *from* Christ, they would indeed help forward this good work."

"Yes, and they would then show more sympathy

to those, who, after having had forty years' hard drinking like my husband, leave it off at one stroke, and bravely and boldly continue to do so in the face of all temptation and jeering."

"It is a noble sight to see any bad habit relinquished; but, Raymond, we must all, as you said just now, *cling to Christ*, and He will help us to give up *every* bad habit, by the power of the Holy Spirit."

And thus we parted with a hearty "God bless you!"

There are several men in our Society who have been stopped in their career of drinking at an equally late season in life.

It is a remarkable fact, that, in no instance, has it injured a man's health to become a total abstainer suddenly. And at this moment, Oct. 1st, 1860, when 450 men are standing firm in our ranks, not one is on the sick-list.

"Lead us not into temptation."

"Woe unto the world because of offences."

CHAPTER VI.

"LET us bear in mind that if the law possesses but little power in compelling to do good, its influence, when wisely directed, is immense in *restraining from evil;* and surely it falls within its legitimate province to surround the people with circumstances that are conducive to good, and to remove, as far as possible, those which are provocatives to evil. The Gospel alone, it is true, can regenerate society; but God has left the task of removing external hindrances in our hands; and we may as well expect to gather grapes of thorns, and figs of thistles, as expect a people to be orderly, temperate, and religious, whom the law has beset with the seductions and stimulants of vice."

I awoke one morning with these words on my mind, and hunting up the old newspaper in which they occur, in a "Letter from a Jail Chaplain," I read them through again and again; until, as we talked it over at breakfast, my thoughts were arrested by a packet of letters from the post, which I had not noticed before.

Amongst them was one from our friend, Edith Somers, enclosing a letter from her cousin, a chaplain in India, to whom she had some time before sent a copy of "Haste to the Rescue."

The letter was dated, "B——, Jan. 19th, 1860," and began as follows:—

"Many thanks for Mrs. W——'s book..... much as your friend knows of the evils arising from drinking in Shrewsbury, even she would be shocked if she saw the state of our military hospitals out here.

"The beds are full of drunkards, or of men whose constitutions have been prepared for every sort of disease by 'moderate' indulgence in spirits for years.

"I have done everything in my power * to rescue members of my flock from the monster evil; but, in the *army*, especially in India, very little success can be expected to result, so long as the GREAT CAUSE is left untouched.

"Many hard-drinking soldiers tell me that they believe they never would have become such, but for the constant supply at hand, which is to be had at the canteen of every barrack at home, and every regimental lines out here.

"Why will Government persist in such a disgraceful system? For the sake of a percentage on the intoxicating liquors, they encourage the premature

* Except the only thing which could meet the case, namely, the total abstinence pledge.

decay, and cause the death of many a soldier, who would otherwise live to serve his Queen and country.

"This is taking the lowest view of the matter—looking at it merely as a question of profit and loss, considering the private soldiers as representing so much of the nation's money." . . .

My heart sickened. I thought of the thousand links in that most complicated chain of separate interests suggested by the words "the Government."

The great brewing interests, the wine and spirit traffic, the immense revenue from the license duty, in fact, the whole of the present licensing system: subjects so intimately bound up with the physical and moral well-being of our nation.

What is to be done when it is a fact that there is hardly a Member of the Cabinet or of Parliament who does not seem to show the most profound ignorance and unconcern about the statistics of intemperance? *Most conscientiously* are the strongest measures passed for increasing the opportunities and facilities for drinking, with the avowed intention of stopping drunkenness, and with the full belief that these measures are adapted for that most desirable end!

What hope have we then from legislative enactments? None at all apparently.

Shall *we*, therefore, fold our arms, and do nothing?

God forbid! There is the more cause for us to be up and doing.

My full conviction is, and it is strengthened every day, that the remedy is in our own hands.

In the face of every obstacle and temptation by which Government surrounds the people, *they* (the people themselves) are *yearning* to cast off the thraldom of *the drink;* and are ready to do so, if only encouraged and strengthened by the sympathy and countenance of those to whom they can look up, and whom they can trust.

Instead, therefore, of mourning over conditions which we cannot at present alter, why should not every one who possesses any influence,—the clergy especially,—use prayerfully and unswervingly the way which is open to them, and which is so simple and easy that even *children* may strengthen our hands by giving their help?

I speak of *the pledge.* Let no one despise it, until he has tried it, or has proved that he can rescue drunkards without it.

How heartily we ought to thank God that the mighty obstacle to all social and moral progress is an EXTERNAL HINDRANCE which *we can take up in our hands and put out of our brother's way.*

The chaplain in India, my friend Edith's cousin, from whose letter I have just quoted, had his attention roused by the *facts*, the successful results of the pledge in our work in Shrewsbury. He could not banish the subject: it was evidently one of vital importance, especially in a climate like India where effects from drunkenness are more quickly fatal.

In his next letter home he wrote thus:—

"February 14th, 1860.

. . . "I enclose a line to let you know that I have become a total abstainer now! After considering the matter again and again, and trying to see it in all its bearings, I have decided to join your side.

"My brother padre, the chaplain to the —— regiment, has joined me, AND WE HAVE ALREADY OBTAINED 250 SIGNATURES TO OUR PAPER! Our first meeting takes place to-night. I will let you know how we get on. It is now a fortnight since I took the pledge, and I must confess that I feel none the worse for total abstinence. Many of the *worst* characters amongst the soldiers, Artillery and Highlanders, have signed. Send me all the tracts on the subject which you come across."

Here is a glorious amount of influence gained in one fortnight, and *by clergymen*, over men hitherto inaccessible to any influence. Henceforth is opened up to these good men a sympathy with the heart of the most abandoned and reckless, who, feeling themselves as "brands plucked from the burning," and, like her to whom much was forgiven, "loving much." will gratefully and affectionately rally round their kind pastors, who have made common cause with them against *their* enemy "*the drink.*" Eternity alone shall tell the result; for a net-work of influences surrounds every person, even the humblest. No one can make a stand against any evil custom or sinful practice, without drawing others insensibly to do the same.

I will venture to say that these two clergymen will henceforth feel there is a depth of meaning, a world of pathos, in these words of our Lord's prayer, "Lead us not into temptation."

Is it not worth making *one* small sacrifice for Christ's sake, to gain such influence over accountable human beings, if haply some erring brother or sister may be rescued from sin and death for life and glory?

Though it should be our lot to stand almost alone amongst those in our own position in this matter, the cold smile, the good-natured banter, or pity of those who differ from us, will hardly be felt as a trial; our hearts will be too full of the sweet music in the altered hearths and homes of our faithful band of total abstainers,—our noble sisters and brothers who have joined our side—to feel otherwise than *intensely* happy. Life is too real, too earnest, to heed anything, however adverse. Through this drink *souls are perishing*,—precious souls for whom Christ died.

Time is fast fleeting away; we dare not stay our hand, if "*by any means we can save some*" dear brother or sister.

It is quite cheering to see how thankfully and bravely our fellow-countrymen of the working classes make a stand against this besetting sin wherever any one will kindly lead them.

The thought forces itself on our minds, Verily it is a healthier token for good to our nation, to see men standing firm in the midst of every besetment and allurement to this vice, than it would be to see Government removing the latter from an unwilling, besotted, and unawakened people.

But, by God's help, WE WILL NOT REST UNTIL WE DO GET THESE HINDRANCES REMOVED; IT IS MOST IMPORTANT.

It is evident that great responsibility rests with the clergy in this matter. If they would rise to the emergency (*would to God they knew the influence they possess!*) there is no hesitation in saying, that, before another generation has passed, drunkenness, if not wholly swept from our borders, would scarcely exist.

In the midst of every discouragement from the Government, we find working men, hitherto sunk for years in this debasing vice, thankfully accept the proffered hand of a brother or sister who feels for their degradation, and is ready to help them out of it. These men have been actors in the scene, and have learned, by sad experience, the appalling havoc made by strong drink in their own homes. They become intelligent and conscientious total abstainers. There is scarcely a man of straw amongst them. They live in the heart of all the old temptations and associations, and they become well-tried veterans, men of strong purpose and resolute will; they eschew the old companions as thoroughly as they do "the drink," unless it be to fulfil the Apostle's words, "Of some have compassion, making a difference; and others save with fear, pulling them out of the fire, hating even the garment spotted with flesh."

John Simmons said to me one evening, "I couldn't help thinking, as we sat at your meeting last night, if you had no other trophies than the five men who sat side by side in that second row, you'd have cause to bless God to all eternity that you ever begun your work amongst us with the temperance pledge."

"Who sat in that row, John?"

"Well, there was myself, and ——"

"Oh! I remember now; all staunch, good men."

"Yes; and to think of us all being what we once was: it's past all belief the change in them four."

"And in *you* also. The grace of God has touched all your hearts."

"Yes, ma'am, *nothing short of that, I am sure.* I could never have kept on for a day, if it hadn't been for His grace, and them words, 'Lead us not into temptation,' which I've prayed twenty times a-day sometimes."

And who were the other four? One is an old man who never used to go to any place of worship. He might have been seen reeling home on his pay-nights, and was sometimes found lying down in the street. Now, God be praised, he has come to Christ. He is never absent from his parish church any Sunday, where he is also a monthly communicant. He always attends our meetings; and it is a wonder if his voice is not heard every Saturday night at the men's prayer-meeting; and if some can express their wants and their praises in more flowing words, no prayers have ever touched our hearts more, or drawn more tears from our eyes, than the prayers uttered by dear old William Fielding. It is no small honour to have been instrumental in rescuing such an one for Christ, to become, as he has done emphatically, "an Israelite indeed, in whom is no guile."

Another is my friend, the author of the letter No. 6, in a previous chapter, as simple-hearted and truthful a man as we have in our ranks. He, too, has become a monthly communicant, and joins in prayer with us on Saturday nights.

When a man was signing the pledge at our house the other day, it was beautiful to hear him giving advice to the new recruit, "You maunna keep on with the old companions. You must give them up.

You must come to the house of God instead, and then you'll hear something that'll touch your heart. You'll soon find out as how you've got no strength; you must pray to the Lord to keep you; and you'll find He will put strength in you. Pray to Him, and He will give you the Holy Spirit to help you."

Both these men gave a touching little speech on receiving from me their twelvemonths' card, by way of encouraging and strengthening their brothers. Of the other two I can speak with the same thankfulness that they also have learned of Christ, and have become other men, though they were once noisy and drunken.

Oh! how I shall bless God through eternity for this little, foolish, despised instrument, the pledge! Verily, it is as unlikely a weapon in the cause of Christ as ever was the jaw-bone of the ass in fighting the Lord's battles against the uncircumcised Philistines. But then it must be used *for Christ*, and not for *secular* social reform alone.

We can testify to the fact that without the pledge our work in Shrewsbury would have been a failure. Not one of the persons now influenced for Christ would have been in the position in which they are. God's blessing has amply rested upon our adoption of the pledge. *To Him be all the praise.*

It is no small thing to feel one's self a rallying point for intelligent and loving human hearts, and to *know* that a bond of union has sprung up of a special kind which shall never be broken; that an element of happiness has been put by God Himself into the eternal future, whose preciousness is beyond all price. God grant us grace to use the influence He gives us for His glory, and not for self. The love of the people is very dear to me, and their prayers revive my heart.

Whilst writing this, another letter from the Chaplain in India has arrived, dated June 26th, 1860, in which, to our great joy, we find the total abstinence pledge is still kept by him and his people.

He writes to his cousin thus: — "You speak of 'sacrifice and inconvenience' attending 'taking the pledge.' I cannot pretend to having experienced either in my own case. . . . . . Taking the pledge has done wonders for some of my flock. I will tell you of one case in particular. S. M. Hoggins, now at this station, had long been a hard drinker, and his commanding officer began to talk of removing him from his appointment. For the sake of Mrs. Hoggins, the wife, an excellent woman, and her large family, many people here had done all they could, in the way of advice and warning, to induce him to give up his ruinous habit of drink. Nothing seemed to have any effect on the man. He would be better for a week or two, and then go back once more to his old ways. He was one of the first to sign the paper. From the day he did so, he became a different man. He assured me yesterday that he never before had such health since he came to India (ten years ago), as he has had since February last. He has now lost all craving for drink, and declares that nothing shall induce him to taste wine, spirits, or beer again, as long as he lives in India. I have now no more regular attendant at church, whenever there is service, than Hoggins, and he is spoken of in the highest terms by his commanding officer. His wife no longer lives in dread of disgrace and penury. On the contrary, there is not a happier, more well-to-do family in B——, than that of S. M. Hoggins. . . . . I must not omit to tell you that two officers of the — Regiment are members of my total abstinence society, both men of high Christian principle. Several more have *almost* given up 'intoxicating beverages,' though they have not put down their names on my list."

Whilst on this subject, I cannot resist adding the testimony of another officer in India, who states that on Lord Keane's return from Affghanistan the supply of rum came to an end. The consequence was, in a week's time, there were not a dozen men sick in the whole camp. The surgeon told the general that he had *not one* man in hospital! This may be called a *speaking* fact.

A letter just received from Bengal closes with the

following words, "The weather here is very trying at present; while I write a *savage* wind is blowing fiery hot from the west. *Still, to-day,* every man *and boy* in the — Regiment is *offered two* 'tots' of raw spirits by the Government! *O tempora! O mores!*"

This needs no comment, after what has been said.

There are solemn aspects in all total abstinence work. Some, who appear for a time to be saved, are again involved in the awful vortex of temptation, and perish without hope. There will always be some who draw back unto perdition. St. Paul speaks of such.

To some, the strong smell of spirits, or malt liquor, in passing a public-house, has much the same effect as a "first glass" would have on others. I know of a man whose name stands high as having written a very telling pamphlet on Total Abstinence who is in this condition. Six times in one fortnight he signed the pledge, and as often broke it. With tears he deplored his inability to refrain, whilst the strong fumes from the beer and spirit houses he passed overcame him at every step, with a power he was utterly incapable of resisting,—it was a disease over which he had no control. Call it what you will, sin or infirmity, ought human beings to be *thus cruelly subjected to temptation,* that they shall not be able to stand, even when their better nature struggles against that special sin? Is it fair? is it right? is it *Christian?* Will not those who love our Lord band themselves together to cast out this abomination from our land, this stumbling-block from our brother's path?

The sense of smell becomes extraordinarily keen in a total abstainer. Shall he therefore be assailed by temptation in a quarter over which he is powerless, when he has done all he can himself do to give up his sin?

"Woe unto the world because of offences, but woe unto him through whom the offence cometh," &c.

Were it not better to cut off the right hand, to pluck out the right eye, than to *countenance* the greatest stumbling-block Satan ever laid before man?

"It is good neither to eat flesh, nor to drink wine, nor any thing whereby thy brother stumbleth, or is offended, or is made weak.

"Wherefore, if meat make my brother to offend, I will eat no flesh while the world standeth, lest I make my brother to offend."

"But," say some people, "why not get these people to be *moderate drinkers?* I consider the moderate drinker takes a higher ground than the total abstainer."

To this I answer, Take facts as they stand, and just lay aside all argument founded on *theory*.

In the abstract I quite agree with you, *provided "the drink" be a harmless or nutritious thing, which I deny.*

But, apply it to life, and you shall soon see the fallacy of your argument.

In the social circle there shall be two men of the same age and position in society; they shall be brothers, breathing the same moral atmosphere, surrounded by the very same influences. The one shall drink without a thought of pleasure, he shall drink fearlessly and freely. No one ever saw him excited; he is unimpassioned and calm; he shall pass for a very moderate man: who can doubt his morality? Who ever saw him excited by drink? The other is a very different person, he is tremblingly alive to every impulse, he is the very soul of the social circle. He shall take one glass, only one. Is it his fault that it shall run through his veins like fire, that the next glass shall effect every nerve in his frame, and make him crave after a third, thus dethroning his moral power, his self-control? and yet this man has taken but two glasses, and is branded as a drunkard, the other shall have taken ten, and is called *moderate.*

Some men cannot stop at the first glass; I know several who cannot. It is no disgrace to them to acknowledge it, and to abstain in consequence of it. It is not their fault so much as the condition of their nervous constitution, unless they have brought themselves into this state through drunkenness.

Again, a working man can hardly be a moderate drinker; it is not *in the nature of the drink* he takes; it is so drugged, that it creates a thirst, and cheats him into drinking more in order to allay it—*fatal delusion!*

Moderate drinkers from amongst these ranks, men who were considered moderate, have told me that their only claim to the title was their staying away from the public-house, for if they went for one glass, resolved to take but one, it was almost sure to be their lot not to stop drinking till they were turned out.

"Granted that it is better the working classes should be total abstainers, you surely would not interfere with the social customs of the educated and the refined?"

My friend, if drunkenness were confined to any one class, the remedy might be safely confined to the same.

But do we not all know gentlemen who never

drink less than a bottle of wine daily? Perhaps, their sons, in following their example, may find it impossible to escape the drunkard's fate. Where is the medical man who does not reckon amongst his patients men of education and position, alas! and *ladies too,* who exceed habitually?

In a recent pamphlet written by a learned Dean, we read that it is no strange thing for ladies to have *delirium tremens.* He has known instances, and so have I.

Are there no young men of hope and promise to whom the "wine-parties" in Oxford have been a snare and trap, the first step to ruin? Are there none who started in life with a thorough distaste for intoxicating drinks, who were betrayed and lost through the usages of society?

I have been entreated by persons of rank and position (personal strangers, whose names are sacred) to receive into our family some loved one, victims of this sad passion; a daughter, once beautiful, elegant, accomplished,—a sister, dearly loved,—a son, once the joy of his mother,—to recover them from the fatal snare by our influence; and it has almost broken my heart to decline the high and holy work; but having my head, hands, and heart fully taxed, what could I say?

It would be well if persons who are sceptical on this subject, could see behind the scenes as we have done, and witness the havoc made by this monster evil in families of different ranks and classes.

To me the subject is become one of the most painful interest. It is fraught with

"Thoughts that do often lie too deep for tears."

It is the strangest delusion that Satan ever yet fastened upon the mind of man, to invest that *dire poison,* which is the most prolific source of sorrow, crime, and disease, in our land, with the life-giving and invigorating properties necessary for a daily beverage, to be fearlessly placed upon the table at every meal, and especially at all our pleasant feasts; alike for the daily use of the strong man, the delicate woman, or the little child.

David Brodie, Esq. M.D., writes thus: "We have wondered what good quality these universal favourites were possessed of, to make them so welcome at almost every board; and, like Diogenes looking for an honest man, we have searched the secret recesses of science, and the busy scenes of every-day life, for anything good, which a healthy man, woman, or child, could get out of these much-loved drinks, but hitherto it has been in vain. We cannot find one single good quality which they possess, to compensate for the load of woes which they inflict upon the foolish family of mankind.

"But some will say, Is not alcohol a medicine? Yes, it is a medicine, and one too which could not well be dispensed with.* But healthy beings don't live upon medicine. Prussic acid, arsenic, and opium, are medicines; yet, would he not be treated as a madman who invited his friends to TAKE A LITTLE OF any of them? So it is with alcohol. It is a medicine, but it is also a *poison*, and, however diluted or disguised it may be, has no quality which can render its administration beneficial, or *otherwise than hurtful* to a healthy frame.

" The stimulating effects which all sorts of alcoholic liquors produce upon the living system, are the great spring of their attractiveness; and the idea is generally cherished that this stimulation is nothing more than a quickening of the vital processes, rousing the various functions into increased activity, and thus adding to the joys of rational existence. The depression which necessarily follows this stimulation is regarded as greatly too small an evil to counterbalance the previous happiness and enjoyment. All the current notions of sociability are pervaded with this absurd and mischievous mistake; and poets and tippling philosophers both have lent their eloquence to embellish the 'joys' of the 'cheering cup' or the 'friendly glass.'

* Some medical men have dispensed with its use for many years.

This strange exciter has been regarded as the only natural source of

"'The feast of reason and the flow of soul.'

"Too many of the great geniuses of whom we are proud, have largely aided in surrounding the drinking customs with this artificial and deceptive halo. But an appeal from the genius in the social group to the genius alone on the coming morrow, if we only had his confessions, would give another view of the question . . . . . .

"Genius is not ennobled, but bedimmed and dishonoured, by its alliance with intoxicating liquors. There is no joy worthy of the name, in any degree of this indulgence. Man is intended to enjoy life, and will have enjoyment; but it is ever and always a bitter and joyless stream which flows from *the spirit bottle*, and abstainers ought not to acknowledge it as gladdening, or represent their abstinence as an act of self-denial."

It has been with me a matter of grave question since I considered the subject seriously, how far it is right for any who draw near to God as ministers of His Word and Sacraments to allow the unhallowed fire of alcohol in any degree to give a false life to their ministrations. Whatever may be their habit at other times, I believe they would have more fruit of their labour if they would, during their attendance in the Sanctuary, entirely abstain from drink, and depend wholly on the quickening power of the Holy Ghost.

It is not *brilliancy* but *earnestness*, kindled by love to Christ and a yearning after souls, which is the secret of all effective and successful preaching.

It is very remarkable that God strictly forbade any priest during the old dispensation, *under pain of death*, to draw near to Him to minister, unless he was, for the time being at least, a total abstainer from all intoxicating drinks.

The same command is renewed in the closing chapters of Ezekiel in reference to those priests who shall minister in that temple which is still a subject of the future.

This proves that *any* degree of fervour or zeal kindled by the unhallowed fire of stimulating drink, in our approaches to God, is abomination in His sight; and it also proves that total abstinence from the same is not unscriptural; though it is nowhere else given as a special command, except to the Nazarite who was from the womb consecrated to the service of God.

Would to God there were none but total abstainers amongst our clergy! If the twenty thousand clergymen of our National Church would stand forth as *protestors* against our national vice by *example and precept*, what a glorious harvest of souls might be gathered in during this generation from amongst a class confessedly now beyond their influence!

And we should see then, no "transgressors in wine," amongst themselves, which, as they are encompassed with like infirmity as other men, is not,—alas! to our sorrow be it said—the case now.

When the trustees of the proposed Inebriate Asylum in New York issued an appeal to the churches of the United States and the American public for assistance, they wrote thus: "Who can doubt the vital importance of such an asylum, when, even before its first story is completed, *many* applications have been made for admittance, a number of which are from the patients themselves? Among the applicants are, 28 clergymen, 36 physicians, 42 lawyers, 3 judges, 12 editors, 4 army, and 3 naval, officers, 179 merchants, 55 farmers, 515 mechanics, and 410 women, *most of them ladies.*"

Harry Stevens.

"Woe unto him that giveth his neighbour drink, that puttest thy bottle to him, and makest him drunken also."

CHAPTER VII.

I WAS wishing to get from Hill's Lane to Barker Street one day, and was sorely puzzled which to choose between two passages which looked very much alike, when, suddenly, I was accosted by an intelligent-looking man. I asked him the way. "This is the right road, ma'am; and, as I am just going the same way myself, I shall be very proud to show you." I perceived it was my friend Harry Stevens, who had lately returned to our ranks.

"Oh, Mr. Stevens! I did not recognise you before. I am so glad of the opportunity of meeting you. Will you let me ask you some questions about your business and its temptations when you have leisure? And may I publish them afterwards?"

"Oh, certainly, ma'am. With great pleasure I will tell you anything you like. I'm heartily sick of the trade, and shall be very thankful to get anything else to do as soon as I can. It's a disagreeable business, and a blackguard one. I detest it!"

"What are you fit for? Because there are

several persons who are willing to take any man I recommend, if they have a vacancy."

"Well; I'm fit for a clerk's place. I could keep any sort of accounts, having had a thoroughly good education."

"Will you come to-morrow night, at eight o'clock, to our house?"

"With much pleasure."

When he came, I asked him how it was he did not continue with us after he signed first, some thirteen months ago.

"Well, ma'am, the fact was, I was calling at a large farmhouse at A——, and Mr. Jones pressed me to drink. I was so resolved not to break the pledge that I refused all malt liquors, wine, and spirits; but when he mentioned cider, I said, 'I believe there is no objection to my taking that.' So I took three half-pints; and when I got home I told George Walmsley what I had done, and he said, 'You are off our list, then, for she don't allow cider to be drunk;' and then, of course, I thought myself out of your Society, and so it was no use to keep strict any longer, as I had broken the rules, so I took anything that offered in the way of drink."

"Well, that is a great pity. If I know that any man in my Society has taken cider *ignorantly*, as you did, I pass it over, on condition that he has taken nothing else, and that he has taken that in moderation. But of course you are aware that men may get very tipsy on cider, and they do so oftener than upon beer or ale in the counties where it is chiefly made."

"Yes, ma'am, I know that; but I should have been very thankful to have stayed in your Society if I had been aware of what you say."

"Were you brought up to your present business of brewing and malting?"

"I was; my father was in it, and my grandfather before him. Grandfather made our business, for he rose from a labouring man, and he married well. We are related to all the best families amongst the tradesmen and farmers in the neighbourhood. In 18— my father died. His estate was greatly embarrassed, and I had some work in getting all straight. In January 18—, the —— Banking Company were in a difficulty through cashiers, who caused defalcations to the bank of a large amount. I had twenty-five shares in the bank, and, trading largely, had got embarrassed. I speculated largely in hops, hoping to retrieve my fortune; but it was a failure, and I lost forty per cent. I got disheartened, and in a low way; my hopes were blighted, and I found myself brought to poverty. So then I took to drink. My malting, ale, and porter business all went wrong, and I got down to the very lowest state."

"I thought that yours was generally considered a very profitable business."

"It's a business that has too many calls upon it for that; and our temptations are tremendous; it is next to impossible to escape being drunkards ourselves. Just to give you an idea, suppose I give you one morning's work, for you to judge of it. Well, suppose it is morning. I'm off early to Ketley to receive orders. It's a black, smoky district, full of iron-works, some of the largest in the kingdom. The poor men who are puddlers or shinglers are continually running in and out of the public-houses to quench their thirst."

"Oh, stop! What are puddlers or shinglers?"

"The men at the furnaces who melt the iron. It's a sight never to be forgotten to see them with the iron in a glowing red liquid state."

"Oh, yes, I know. I have seen them at Wednesbury, at Mr. Lloyd's works."

"The men are almost naked at their work; they have dark woollen trousers, but not a rag besides. They sweat dreadfully, and they get awfully thirsty; poor fellows! they will drink from two to three gallons of porter apiece daily, and I don't know how much water besides. They get from five to six shillings a-day; at forty-five or fifty years of age they are incapacitated for labour; for all they sweat so dreadfully, they get very bloated and stout."

"Of course they do, like the men employed in the brewery business in London; the porter makes them so; but they are not strong for all that."

"No; or they would not have to give up work at that age. Well, then; you see I arrive early in the morning at John Thompson's, the landlord of the Nag's Head in Ketley (I don't give the right names, but I will if you wish), and I ask what orders he has for me; how much malt he'll have?"

"'Well, Mr. Stevens, right glad to see you to-day. Come and have a glass?'

"'No, indeed. Can't drink so early in the day, much obliged to you all the same.'

"'Then, if you won't drink, I'll give you no order.'

"I remonstrate with him.

"'I've put your name down for a shilling, Mr. Stevens, towards a raffle; now, you must be social, man, and take your glass, or there's no orders for you; I mean it.'

"The landlord is *fresh*, and he will not take a denial, he gets clamorous. I yield, take one glass, we go on to a second, and I drive my bargain. We go on drinking till I get half drunk. I get an order for twenty or thirty pounds' worth of malt; then the customers come in, and I must be bound to treat them. Then the old brewing woman comes in, and must have her share, too. And this has to be repeated at every public-house in Ketley; and, remember it 's before dinner, on an empty stomach. I am getting half tipsy before I leave the first house."

"Oh! how shocking!"

"It is. It 's awful for soul and body, and I cannot stand it any longer. Then, in three months' time, I have to call again, the accounts have become due. They will have three months; but the farmers won't give us maltsters more than a fortnight, and then there's the duty for the Queen. The fact is, the brewer and maltster has to find the capital for the publicans to work upon; four-fifths of them have no capital at all. Well, I go to John Thompson's again for the bills. I present them for payment, 'Well, what will you have?' is the first question from the landlord. The missus keeps me waiting a long time, very reluctant to pay. Then a clandestine message is sent off to the customers, and they come swarming in to be treated. I am thought very shabby if I don't spend a shilling or two upon them. And then the landlord, before he pays me, exposes the bank-notes to the company, who look upon it as a clear profit. Then I have to make a discount of two and sixpence on every twenty bushels (we get but one shilling by the farmers for the same); and then, besides that, I have to treat and to spend with the landlord (say) half-a-crown more. And this, as before, has to be repeated at every public-house. And by night you may suppose what sort of a condition one is in."

"Well, you are not working on your own account now; do you find that you lose orders from public-houses by being a total abstainer?"

"Of course, they don't like it. I throw down my sixpence now, instead of drinking. I have been employed by Mr. Sinclair since March. He gives me a guinea a-week, and pays my travelling expenses. I have sold 120*l.* worth of oil-cakes, a quantity of manure, and 150*l.* worth of ale and porter. That's not bad for two months' canvassing!"

"When did you come to Shrewsbury?"

"In March 18—. I had no friend, all my old companions turned their backs upon me, I was destitute, broken-hearted. You will have an idea how reduced I was when I tell you that I pawned my watch and the ring I had worn in my gay days! I used to have 400*l.* a-year in my malting and porter business, when I was hop and seed merchant, too. I kept a horse then for business, and a good one he was, for I often used him for hunting. I kept a good house in those days,—open house, I mean, and treated my friends to parties,—supper-parties chiefly, when we used to have cards, &c. Ah, it was a different thing when I came to Shrewsbury destitute, no one would know me; those persons who had been my guests many a time turned their backs upon me, or scarcely took notice of me. And there's a member of the Rifle

Corps I met to-day, he would hardly deign to look at me."

After a few kind words of sympathy, we began to talk about the adulterations in beer and porter, whereupon my friend told me the following story:—

"A customer of mine, at —— (he had been huntsman to a gentleman) took to a little beer-house, and I supplied him entirely with malt and hops. I was at his house one day, and drunk two glasses of ale, after which I went to two other houses which I served, and drank the same quantity at each. It did not take effect instantly, but shortly after a violent giddiness came over me and an awful thirst, head burning with excitement, hot as possible. I went to the principal inn, and was completely delirious, and began piling up the chairs one upon another. The landlady came and remonstrated with me, but she saw I was ill, and she sent me home in the care of the ostler. Next morning I had racked head, bloodshot eyes, and was quite ill. I took soda-water and exercise, which brought me round, but left me very weak. The excise-officer detected grains of paradise in the boiler where the ale was boiling at those three houses! They were asked how it came there; one of them answered, he supposed it must have come in the malt from Mr. Stevens. The officer called upon me as a matter of course, but, as he told me, he knew very well I had nothing to do with it. The bench inflicted a penalty of 100*l.* upon each of the three landlords; but at the instigation of friends the fine was reduced to 25*l.*, and one of them came to borrow the money of me to pay it!"

He then told me that grains of paradise are used by poachers in catching fish. "I have used them myself for that; the way is this, the grains are bruised, mixed with flour and water, and rolled out like paste, and then made into little balls or pills with the palms of the hand. If you throw them on the water, the fish come and nibble at them, and each one is seized with giddiness, and whisks round and round, and then in a moment floats on his back, and you take them out with your hand, as easy as possible. I have done it myself."

"This must be quite a poison."

"It very nearly killed me. But I am now solemnly purposed to be a very different man, and to spend *my Sundays*, above all, very different to what I've done, for I have been going on very rackety now for a long time," (he meant, before he signed again.)

"Oh, Mr. Stevens, come heartily to our dear Saviour; all the reformation that is merely outward will go for nothing; if you stay away from Him, it can only be outward."

"I never was for outside change: I hate hypocrisy."

"I didn't mean to think for a moment you wish to appear what you are not. I only mean to say, we *may* become moral outwardly without having one spark of love to Jesus. Come to Him, for nothing short of this is religion; nothing short of this will give you what you want, a Friend in sorrow and trial, a Saviour to wash away all your sins, and bring you faultless into the presence of God."

"I will,—indeed, I will, for I am sick of the past altogether."

"God bless you!"

And we parted; but just before he left, I asked if he understood fully that I wanted to publish all he had said to me, and would he give his consent?

"Yes, most willingly; and if you wish to know anything further about the business, I will tell you to the best of my power. But tobacco is used for adulterations, and other things, too."

"O yes! I know that, but *this* is new to me, about the grains of paradise."*

Now, after this, I ask, what Christian man would be a maltster and brewer?

The evil does not end here. The men employed in making the malt are occupied from six to eight months every year, working during that time as much

* And yet I might have known, for similar cases of fining before the magistrates occur constantly, and are named in the public papers.

on Sundays as on any other day in the week. They can make no difference, for malt cannot be made without eight continuous days.

It is computed that there are 40,000 working men thus employed in the kingdom, utterly deprived of their Sabbaths. If it can be proved that the making of malt is a work of *mercy* or *necessity* the question is at an end.

But, for what purpose is the malt employed? For the manufacture of intoxicating drinks, such as ale, porter, and gin, in purchasing which, the working man, "for every shilling he pays to the publican, obtains but one pennyworth of *nutrition* in return! How much more *mercy* would there be in providing him with beef-steaks, mutton-chops, and rashers of bacon, fed with the barley thus expensively cooked, when every morsel would tell as nourishment, and the man would have twelve-pennyworths for his shilling!"*

Barley, in the degree of nourishment it contains, is next to wheat. Sir Humphry Davy ascertained that 1000 parts of barley contain 920 parts that are nutritive, but when made into malt the most substantial part of the malt is left in the grains and given to the pigs, or found at the bottom of the cask after the beer has been drawn off.

"The quantity of grain destroyed annually," says

* From No. 7, Ipswich Temperance Tracts.

the author of "Anti-Bacchus," "in converting it into intoxicating drink, would, according to parliamentary calculations, support about a twelfth part of our inhabitants throughout the year; forty millions of bushels of malt, at eight shillings per bushel, are worth sixteen millions sterling; and supposing bread to be eightpence the quartern loaf, *sixteen millions* sterling would purchase *three thousand eight hundred and forty millions* of quartern loaves, and consequently would supply upwards of *two millions* of persons with *two pounds of bread per day for a whole year.*"

But the destruction of God's good gift, the grain, is only the beginning of the mischief. The brewer and distiller then have their part to act by supplying those beverages which man calls "refreshment," but which God has branded with the character of at the last "biting like a serpent and stinging like an adder." Emphatically are they the curse of England, turning kind husbands and fathers, and tender wives and mothers, into worse than brutes, licentious fiends; and filling our gaols, workhouses, and lunatic asylums, with degraded specimens of fallen humanity.

I read in a London paper to-day the following Parliamentary statistics:—

"For the year ending at Michaelmas last (1859), 56,161 persons in England and Wales were punished by magistrates for being drunk, or drunk and disorderly, 10,486 of them women; the number charged was 89,903, of whom 24,395 were women. In 306 cases, in the year 1859 on coroners' inquests, a verdict was found of 'Died from excessive drinking.'"

In the year 1854, in England and Wales alone, there were 89,866 public-houses, and 41,547 beer-shops. Who licensed all these? Are the magistrates ignorant of the fact, that nearly every public-house in the kingdom is open (in a way understood by the customers) during the illegal hours for traffic of intoxicating drinks, *every Sunday throughout the year?* Ought the laws of our country to be outraged thus? To whom can we apply for redress, when the protectors and executives of the law are ignorant of facts or tardy in enforcing obedience to those laws?

God help our working classes in such a state of things, and raise up some loving, sympathizing friend, round whom they may rally, in every town and village in the kingdom! And if clergymen and laymen do not stand up for their sake, may women do so, rather than that souls should perish for whom Christ died!

It was stated in the papers that "the murderer Twigg, when in Stafford gaol, waiting his trial for the wilful murder of his wife, at Bilston, in that county, wrote two letters to his relations, who have now the charge of his children, in which he refers, with poignant feelings, to the cause to which his crime is traceable. He tells his children 'never to look at drink and liquors, to knock off bad company. and prepare to meet God, for their wicked, drunken father's sake.' To his wife's brother he writes, 'I hope when your family and mine see liquors and drink, they will take it to be a sting from a serpent, for my sake.' In the second letter he four times refers to the 'drink and liquors' as having influenced him to murder his wife, whom he calls his 'tender bosom friend.' Again, 'for his sake,' he urges his 'butty workmen never to look at drink nor liquors;' and concludes by saying, 'God knows, I little thought I should have been snatched away like this through drunkenness.'"

I will close this chapter with an extract from a letter received by me from the matron of a Refuge in the great metropolis. In speaking of the unfavourable cases, she writes thus:—

"I enclose a few cases, by which you will see that a return to habits of intemperance have been the cause of a relapse into degradation and crime.

"I might multiply cases to a painful extent, but perhaps the few sent will suffice to show how valuable an aid teetotalism would be to the prevention of crime. Nearly all the prisoners who, from time to time, come under my charge (making a daily average of about 172), attribute their fall, in the first instance, to love of drink, and its attendant evil, bad company. You are at liberty to make what use you like of the extracts, or of my letter."

Facts versus Theory.

“Facts are stubborn chiels,
I' faith ye canna ding them.”

CHAPTER VIII.

One day, in passing the Grammar-schools, Richard Daniels, the tailor, accosted me. I congratulated him on his health and strength.

"Yes, ma'am; I never was better in my life."

"And yet this cold February is enough to try one's teetotalism, they tell us! It is bitterly cold, certainly."

"Well, I think it agrees with me. I never was better in my life."

"Would you mind telling me some facts about your past life, to help forward a brother in the right path? I want to publish it for the good of other men in your position."

"No, indeed; I'd tell you anything I know about myself, if it would do anybody good to hear it."

"Oh, thank you. Will you come to our house on Wednesday night after church?"

"Well, I can't answer for that; I may be engaged. You know our trade is very uncertain. Us tailors have little or nothing to do on Mondays; but, towards the middle of the week, a job might chance to drop in of an evening, and then, if it was wanted, we should

be bound to sit up half the night over it, if it was not finished."

"If you are not likely to do anything to-day, it being Monday, suppose you come to me at three o'clock; I shall be at home, and it will suit me perfectly."

After we parted, I mused, as I hastened on in my work, on the idle Mondays of the tailors.

These men are a remarkable class. They are highly intelligent, many of them are well read, and can converse on a variety of subjects. They are very strong in politics; and some of them would make capital members of a debating society, being good speakers. They sometimes work together in companies of fifty. They are a kind-hearted set of men, but, alas! terribly drunken. They seldom, if ever, attend any place of worship. There are a large number working in Shrewsbury; from amongst these several are members of our Society, all firm, steadfast men, who have to stand their ground amongst their drinking companions, and in the midst of all the old associations.

It is easy to see why tailors have nothing to do on Mondays. It is not much use to prepare work for men who, by the Sunday's excesses, are not in a condition to do it. The sober men, being terribly in the minority, have to bear the trial of idle Mondays with the rest.

Punctual to his appointment, my friend came at three o'clock. I honoured the noble and manly frankness with which he answered all my questions, and allowed me access to the facts of his past life for the good of other working men.

"I want, first, to know what sort of early training you had, Mr. Daniels. Did you ever attend a Sunday-school?"

"Yes, ma'am; till I was eighteen years of age I went every Sunday twice to church and to school; I don't know as I ever missed. We lived at Bangor then; and the Rev. Mr. Davies was clergyman at the church I attended."

"What did you do when you were eighteen?"

"Why, I left home, and went to Oswestry, where I had my first start in life as a journeyman tailor. I was more my own master then in the choice of my companions, and the way I spent my leisure hours. It would be a great blessing if some one would look after the young men who are beginning life, and give them a helping hand to spend their time different to what I did. And now I am going to tell you something I want you to make a very strong point of, that is, the *moderate* drinking. I had never drunk anything hardly but water in my life up to this time; but I began in Oswestry to drink a little beer and ale, or anything else that offered; and I made a resolution in myself to restrict it to a pint at a time, and made a rule never, on no occasion, to go beyond that. I little thought it would be hard to keep to it, or what it might lead me to in the end. I didn't know that I had got on a sliding path, though I might have known that I didn't need to begin drinking, as I had done very well without it all my life. You see it was *the company* in the first place. I wished to be like other young men, and, having no friend to take any interest in me, I got into a good bit of company to pass the time at nights. I got amongst lawyers' writing clerks, shopmen, and such like; especially there was a young man, who was serving at a druggist's; he was a great companion of mine. And thus we went to many parties, and chiefly at Christmas, and often I found my rule very inconvenient; so I broke through it occasionally. But, as I kept tolerably steady on the whole, I felt satisfied, though I must confess it got more frequent that I took too much drink, and made too free."

"How long did you live in Oswestry?"

"Two years, and then I came to Shrewsbury. I was twenty years of age now, and, I am ashamed to say, *I got thoroughly into it*, and broke through every restraint. At our trade a man, to work well, must be sober; he cannot do it properly if he has the drink in him. I'll tell you what I've done whilst sitting all day at my work, and those who worked with me will know it to be a fact. After having had *a spree*, I've come so ill to my work, obligated to work to earn something, and so unfit for it, that I've drunk upwards of fourteen half-pints in the day to keep me up to the mark. As the drink kept dying in me, *I was dying*, as it were; and in that state I couldn't have kept up to the mark without the stimulus, though I knew all the while it helped to make me worse afterwards: but it couldn't go on long this way without me being downright ill at last. There are two things I want you to state clearly, for it is an important fact for all working-men to consider; there are two losses a man incurs when he is drinking—*the time* he loses and *the money* he spends—the first is as serious as the other; it's *a double loss.*"

"How old were you when you married?"

"I was twenty-seven. Ah! it's a bad look-out for a woman to marry a man who drinks. I had become a drunkard before I married, but I got much worse afterwards; I drank harder all the while; my faith in moderate drinking was quite gone."

"The same as with many others, I suppose!"

"Yes indeed, ma'am, what is called a sober man amongst us is just one who does not show what he has taken, though at the same time he may have had enough to make half-a-dozen other men quite drunk. I knew a man who was reckoned a very sober man; nobody could ever say he was the worse for drink. When I sat fuddling at a public-house, I have seen that man come in and out to take half-a-pint, and I counted one day just to see what he could take: he drank, to my certain knowledge, eleven half-pints of ale in a morning. Now there's many a man I know would have been reeling about the streets if he had taken half that. *He is dead now;* he was sexton at St. ——'s church."

"I am not surprised to hear he is dead, the *effects* are as sure as if he had appeared tipsy."

"Do you know, ma'am, I once got frightened enough about myself to sign the pledge! and I kept it about ten months, but it was a very different sort of a thing to joining your Society. There was no one to notice us if we kept it or not, so it wasn't much encouragement; and another thing, it was not followed up with religious meetings, so I dropped out of it again after ten months. It was a pain in the chest caused me to sign; it came over me like spasms. I know it was the effect of hard-drinking; just as if one had thrust a sword through me. I remember going to the doctor one day about it; I could hardly bear myself, it was so terrible, and I thought to get rid of it; so I took a glass of hot brandy and water on the way to deaden it; but it made it much worse: and I remember quite well the doctor saying, 'You are adding fire to fire by taking spirits.'"

"You must have seen sad sights in your drinking days at the public-houses?"

"Yes, and some rum ones too sometimes. I remember once seeing all the little pigs in a pig-pen drunk! leaping about like mad; how we all laughed; there's none of us will ever forget the sight; two of them leaped right over the stile into a culvert, and the men were two hours getting them out. The landlord of the public-house got quite angry because he found that the bottoms of the barrels had been thrown into the pigs' wash, and he ordered the wash to be thrown away. You see, ma'am, *he didn't think it was good for strengthening and fattening his pigs,* yet he used to sell that very stuff to us men when we got too drunk to discern what we drank, *and the publicans sell the same now to be made into porter.*"

This reminded me of what a man once told me who had been for many years servant at a gin-palace in London. I chanced to meet him as a stranger at a house when I was visiting a sick person. He assured me, that the publicans gave to their customers, when they were not capable of discerning, *the washings of the barrels,* "stuff we would not give our pigs to eat," as he said; but he defended the custom, saying, "If we'd let them have the real stuff to the last it would kill them; so what are we to do? they *will* keep on asking for drink to the last." And no wonder, poor fellows! the drink they get only adds to their thirst, and makes them mad to appease it; and then, like the poor moth that has singed its wings, they go back to the fire that has half killed them, for relief from the agony.

Now the value of this conversation is just this, that *it is a fact from life*—not an isolated case either, but, as we shall presently show, a sample of almost every tailor's life and career in England. Will any one be stirred up to care for the young apprentices and lads who live close to their own doors? How much sorrow, sin, and misery, might then be prevented! How many wives and children might have happy homes! If drunkenness had not entered to make many a fair home in England a "Ragged Home," we need not now be setting our wits to find out "how to mend them." Prevention is better than cure.

A few days after this conversation, I received from Tunbridge Wells an anonymous manuscript extract from a lecture on "Great Cities and their Influences for Good and Evil," delivered by the Rev. Charles Kingsley, at Bristol, Oct. 1857, which, being very interesting, as bearing on this subject, I transcribe literally.

"I am one of those who cannot, on scientific grounds, consider drunkenness as a *cause* of evil, but as an *effect*. Of course it is a cause—a cause of endless crime and misery; but I am convinced that to *cure*, you must inquire not what *it* causes, but what *causes it;* and for that we have not far to seek. The main exciting cause of drunkenness is, I believe firmly, bad air and bad lodging.

"A man shall spend his days between a foul alley, where he breathes sulphuretted hydrogen, a close workshop where he breathes carbonic acid, and a close and foul bedroom, where he breathes both. For neither of the three places, in the meanwhile, has he any fair share of that mysterious chemical agent, without which health is impossible, the want of which betrays itself at once in the dull eye, the sallow cheek, viz. *light.* Believe me, it is no mere poetic metaphor which connects in Scripture light with life. It is the expression of a deep-laid fact, one which holds as true in the physical as in the spiritual world; a case in which (as perhaps in all cases) the laws of the visible world are the counterparts of those of the invisible world, and earth is the symbol of heaven.

"Deprive, then, the man of his fair share of fresh air and pure light, and what follows? His blood is not properly oxygenated, his nervous energy is depressed, his digestion impaired, especially if his occupation be sedentary or requires much stooping, and the cavity of the chest thereby becomes contracted, and for that miserable feeling of languor and craving he knows but one remedy—the passing stimulus of alcohol—a passing stimulus leaving fresh depression behind it, and requiring fresh doses of stimulants, till it becomes a habit, a slavery, a madness.

"Again, there is an intellectual side of the question. The depressed nervous energy, the impaired digestion, depress the spirits. The man feels low in mind as well as in body. Whence shall he seek exhilaration? Not in that stifling home which has caused the depression itself. He knows none other than the tavern and the company which the tavern brings; God help him!

"Yes, ladies and gentlemen, it is easy to say, God help him! but it is not difficult for man to help him also. Drunkenness is a very curable malady. The last fifty years have seen it all but die out amongst the upper classes of this country. And what has caused the improvement?

"Certainly, in the first place, the spread of education. Every man now has a hundred means of rational occupation and amusement, which were closed to his grandfather. . . . We can find plenty of amusement now, besides the old one of sitting round the table and talking over wine. Why should not the poor man share in our gain?

"But, over and above, there are causes simply physical. Our houses are better ventilated. The stifling old four-post bedstead has given place to the airy and curtainless one, and, what is more than all, *we wash.* That morning cold bath, which foreigners consider as Young England's strangest superstition, has done as much, believe me, to abolish drunkenness as any other cause whatsoever. With a clean skin in healthy action, and nerves and muscles braced by a sudden shock, men do not crave for artificial stimulants. I have found that, *cæteris paribus*, a man's sobriety is in direct proportion to his cleanliness.* I believe it would be so in all classes, had they the means.

"And they ought to have the means. Whatever other rights a man has, or ought to have, this at least he has, if Society demands of him that he should earn his own livelihood, and not be a torment and burden to his neighbour. He has a right to water, to air, and to light. In demanding that, he demands no more than Nature has given to the wild beasts of the forest. . . . . .

"Ragged Schools, Reformatories, Hospitals, and Asylums, treat only the *symptoms, not the actual causes of the disease;* and that the causes are only to be touched by improving *the simple physical conditions of the class;* by abolishing foul air, foul lodgings, and overcrowded dwellings. You may breed a pig in a sty, and make a learned pig of him after all; but you cannot breed a man in a sty, and make a learned man of him, or in any true sense of the word a man at all."

* I believe rather a man's cleanliness is in direct proportion to his sobriety!

I felt sorely puzzled after reading this; puzzled with the FACTS around me, for I could not make them correspond with the theory in this extract. And yet, if I could put my facts clean out of sight, I could go heartily and wholly with every word I read in it. It is all quite true, but not the whole truth.

Pure water, air, and light, who can overrate them? God's beautiful and free gift to all His creatures, which cannot be withheld without peril, I might almost say, of a man's *soul;* for such is the power of the *body over the mind*, of which we hear less said than the *power of the mind over the body*, though it is not a less mighty truth.

Yet, to my mind, it does not solve the mystery: go to facts again. Who is there that cannot point out, even in these days of recreation and science, many who "err through strong drink," in the very highest ranks of educated life? Where is the medical man who does not mourn over *many of his first-class patients, alas! not even excepting ladies*, who have imbibed the fatal passion in spite of airy apartments, plentiful supply of the purest water, and every condition of health, elegance, and refinement? Is it true that drunkenness has almost died out amongst the upper classes?

Would to God that it had done so!

Whilst thinking of facts *versus* theory, Tom Williams called to speak to me. Finding that it was not a busy day with him, I laid the matter before him, saying, "You know more about the subject than I do. Your experience will be valuable to me." (I read the extract to him.) "And now, tell me, what do you think of Mr. Kingsley's view of the main cause of drunkenness?"

"It's very good up to a certain point. But it won't do altogether; *it contradicts facts;* at least, with tailors, shoemakers, and, I suspect, with most of us working-men; for, just look at the bricklayers and farm-labourers, the stone-masons, and sawyers, who don't work in bad air—why, they are all pretty much of a piece. We are most of us drunkards, all of us working-men throughout England; tailors and shoemakers do work in close rooms, that's a fact, but I believe there's not one of them but became drunkards before they felt much effects from them. *It's free and easy company does it:* and not that of itself, it's the company we meet with, *in the midst of the temptations to drunkenness which surround us in our youth at every step.*"

Ah! those temptations to drunkenness! the customs and usages of society, and the public-houses at every turn and corner, and at the entrance of every alley.

In Shrewsbury there are, I am told, 143 inns, hotels, &c., and 68 beer-houses. If the receipts of the former were estimated at 10*l.* weekly, it would give an annual expenditure of 74,360*l.* If the receipts of the beer-houses were estimated at 4*l.* weekly, the annual sum spent would be, 14,144*l.*, giving as the total annual expenditure in the town of Shrewsbury, 88,504*l.* And who spends this money? The working classes alone, or chiefly.

If the Government desired to make a nation of drunkards, it has verily gone the truest way to work to gain that result.

Tom Williams was evidently in a brown study as well as myself. I asked him, "Will you give me a history of your past life? I mean, with a view to publish it, therefore you are to do just as you like about telling me. I wish to do good to other men by relating *facts* which may be a warning and a help to them."

"I will tell you anything you wish, with all my heart, but I must consider a bit. Where shall I begin?"

"Were you ever at a Sunday-school?"

"Oh, yes, a Baptist and Methodist Sunday-school. My parents were both pious, and took care that I went to chapel twice every Sunday. There is just one thing I should wish you to mention particularly. With all their strictness in other things, I was let have my own way in one particular,—I had the free use of our table-beer barrel at home, and that was the beginning of my ruin."

"Then it was not the *publican's beer* which first led you to drink! That is worth recording!"

"No, it was not. Well, we lived at ——, and I continued at home till I was seventeen; at that age I came to Shrewsbury, and worked at Mr. ——'s. I was a professing Christian then, but being my own master, in lodgings, and having a great turn for singing, and being considered a good hand at a comic song, I used to get invited out a great deal, and got into company with *free-and-easys,* fast shopmen, chiefly drinking and gambling, till it led to the quenching of every religious thought. Yet, even then, I had a hard struggle to get rid of conscience. I sometimes prayed and wept; and then again I fell back. And thus I continued sinning and repenting, until at last I became a regular drunkard."

"But you have forgotten your marriage, Williams. When did that take place?"

"When I was twenty-one years of age. Ah, and she was a *Christian woman.* She is now in eternity." Here the past swept over his memory, and with choked voice and eyes full of tears, he added:—

"'She was my angel, my love, and my pride,
Vainly from ruin to save me she tried.
Poor broken-hearted! 'twas well that she died
Long, long ago!'"

After a silence of some minutes, I asked, "Am I to write all you have said?"

"Yes; it may be a warning to others."

He resumed after a while, "Four years after I married again, and we had four children. When one of my little ones was lying in the last stage of consumption, I sought relief for my anguish in drink, for I loved my child to my heart; it was an awful way to quench sorrow, but I had departed so from God, I dared not face Him. I remember she fixed her large soft eyes on me so beseeching, and looking full at me, she said, 'Oh, father, don't get drunk any more!' Oh, that was a bitter cup to me, it was a heavy sorrow."

"How old was she?"

"She was seven. Well, I lost her. . . . . I was reduced to utter poverty. I kept a public-house for two years."

"A public-house! Oh, do tell me your experience as landlord. Where was it?"

"In the suburbs. It was then I got most reduced. Be sure you make that clear, for it's worth knowing that the *Sunday* trading did it. You see, this was the way of it; we got more customers on Sundays than all the week together, and they would stop till their money was all gone, and then we could not turn them out, as the hours were illegal, and so they continued drinking without paying anything at all."

"But could you not summon them for payment?"

"Oh, no! don't you see, it was illegal altogether

my keeping the house open on Sunday; if I had laid any complaints against them, I should have committed myself at the same time! All the publicans nearly carry on the same game now, but no one informs against it, or takes any notice of it."

What is the use of having laws?"

None at all, if they are defied every day."

He then told me to put down how 2*s.* 3½*d.* served him for a week's keep, when all his effects were sold, and he was in his utmost depth of poverty:—

I had

	s.	*d.*
Monday, soup and tobacco . .	0	3½
Tuesday, bread, herring, and coffee .	0	4
Wednesday, soup, coffee, and bread .	0	5½
Thursday, soup, herring, and bread .	0	5½
Friday and Saturday, ditto . .	0	9
	2	3½

"What did your wife live upon that week?"

"Indeed I didn't know. She went to some friend, I think. And yet, when I got any wages, I would again spend nearly the whole of it in drink; all the others I worked with did the same. Was it not wonderful that in my degradation, God never would let me alone, but again and again stirred up my conscience, and sent His Holy Spirit to strive with me; and I would weep and pray, and then sin and forget? Now I want you to make this next a strong point. *I tried to be moderate over and over again,* but I could not be moderate; *each time I tasted I broke down again.* And so it went on, till my poor wife had a sad home of it, and a wretched life. At last, one Sunday night, January 9th, 1859, I went to drown my thoughts, as usual, in drink—came home tipsy. I was ill Monday; returned to the same Tuesday. At night my poor wife and little girl were at their wits' end what to do; they led me to your house to sign. I was so drunk I could not walk without help."

"Am I to write all this?"

"Yes; it will show it's never too late to mend."

"Ah, dear friend, I know all the rest; poor fellow! you stood inside our door. I was at the school-room, engaged at the meeting. You entreated Mr. Wightman to let you sign the pledge. He refused, because you were not sober. We have never refused any one since for that reason. You then said to my husband, 'You will not refuse to pray for me?' and you pulled him down on his knees, just where he stood by the front door. And he knelt down on the door-mat and prayed for you. Next evening (Wednesday) you came to our church, we noticed a man's voice joining in the singing; and I remember well the beadle saying, as we came out of the church, 'Well, ma'am, this is the most wonderful thing of all; here is Tom Williams in church, and of a week night, too!' But I answered, 'There is no man of that name in our Society.' I remember your following us out of church, and telling us that you were the man who came to our house the night before, and then I was so *very thankful* to receive you."

"Ah, God's mercies are boundless! He has kept me until now from that awful drink which for so many years kept me from Him. Heaven helps them as tries to help themselves."

"Yes; God has indeed shown wonderful love and forbearance to every one of us. Really, when I look at you and Richard Daniels, and nearly 200 others, not men only, but also women, I am overwhelmed at His goodness to you and to me."

"Yes, indeed, there's good reason for it; it's not only that we have been kept from the drink, and attending twice at church every Sunday since, and to your meetings, but it is that we have learned we have no strength in ourselves; and we have felt our utter sinfulness also, and have come to Christ to be saved *from* our sins, and to be washed in His blood."

"Ah! that's the best part of it all—the only thing that will ever *satisfy* me. But now, do tell me, how is it that, brought up as a Dissenter, you did not go back to the chapel when you went back to God?"

"Well, it was for a straightforward reason. I'll soon tell you how it was. No one took any notice of me when I fell at my chapel; they left me to myself and Satan. No one took me by the han l, and lifted me from drunkenness, which was at the root of all my degradation and misery, till you and Mr. Wightman did. Oh! if it had but been done twenty years ago! What sin I should have been spared! If the chapel people had done so, I should have continued amongst them to this day; but now I will never go from you as long as I live. I began to attend your church at once, and I shall continue a member of the Church of England as long as I live."

Here is a lesson taught by my grateful friend, how the poor broken heart feels sympathy and kindness—a helping hand when he is down in the mire. Oh, if our blessed Lord had not come down from His throne to this fallen world, where should we all have been? What "beggar from the dunghill" would ever have been raised to "the throne of glory?" He gives us an example by His love, pity, and mercy, which by His grace we may in our measure follow.

True, well-ventilated houses are most necessary for health. Light, air, and fresh water, are God's cheap and great gifts to man; they are *every man's birthright.* Love of money ought not to deprive any man of them.

But no mere physical condition, strongly as it may affect our moral being, is a sufficient reason to account for any SIN. *If there were no root of sin,* no evil, corrupt nature, there would be no branches bearing deadly fruit. The cause lies deep. Man, unconverted man, yearns for something, for some one, to fill the void in his heart which none can fill but God Himself. Thus unsatisfied, he slakes his thirst at every polluted stream, which, failing to satisfy him, only renders the craving more intense. And thus reckless company, mad mirth, and the ready public-house, are the snares which entrap our dear brothers and sisters of the working classes; and, before they are aware of it, the drunkard's thirst is formed; and before the Gospel can reach one who is established in *that sin which is twofold, physical and moral,* a physical remedy, as well as a spiritual remedy, must be applied; even as, before you would preach Jesus to a deaf man, you would remove his impediment by teaching him letters, whereby the sense conveyed to your mind by sound may reach him by some other avenue, so you must remove the external hindrance of drink before you can reach the understanding or heart of a drunkard. You must get him in a *sane* state to hear the Gospel.

Tom Williams and Richard Daniels still work under their different masters, in crowded rooms, with many men. The former was for some time *alone* in religion and total abstinence amongst his set. "Is not this a brand plucked from the burning?" If any one could hear him join with us at our Saturday night prayer-meetings, they would not say that total abstinence had brought him from Christ. It has removed that hindrance which blocked up Christ from his heart; and I bless God for his wife's testimony to the present happiness and peace of her home, ever since January, 1859.

John Ithell is as remarkable a case as any I know amongst the tailors. He and his wife called together one day on me, and we fell into conversation,—so thrilling, that I begged leave to use it, which they most readily granted. I read it to them afterwards, to ensure a correct transcript.

Until fourteen years of age he was a regular attendant at St. ——'s Sunday School, in Shrewsbury. His father was a tailor, a drunken man, much the same as others of his trade. He died when John was seventeen. And now poor John's battle of life began. It was a hard struggle for him, the eldest of seven, to maintain them all, and his mother a widow. For the first twelvemonths he worked in the country; he came after that to reside in Shrewsbury, and got work at Mr.——'s, where fifty men worked in the same shop.

"Ah! that first Saturday night after I came to work in Shrewsbury, I shall never forget it the longest day I live. The men all went to the public-house with their wages; and I had to call for my first pint of beer as I ever drank in my life. I was dreadful ashamed about it. It's a lesson to youth; *all depends on the company they keep at the first starting in life.* I was then in for it, to be as bad as the rest. I fell to attending public-houses, till I lost all shame about it, playing at skittles, and dice, and dominoes, and cards, drinking hard and gambling. Thus it crept over me. I continued a tidyish young man outwardly till I was twenty-three years of age; but I had got on a sliding path, and there was no remedy."

"You were not so rough then as you got afterwards," said his wife.

"No, no; it's age, and drinking so much, as brings that on. But now, I got worse and worse gradually; and at twenty-seven I remember we got drinking one Sunday to a great degree, and three of us started off on tramp to Birmingham. My poor mother was in a great taking about me; and one of us three was a married man with children. We got at last to Birmingham; and the man who had left his wife fell to crying, so he went back to Shrewsbury, and left us at Birmingham."

"Did you get work at Birmingham?"

"Oh, yes, I soon got work; but I never kept it long. The first shop I got work at the wages was paid at a public-house, and as I and the young fellow that came on tramp with me lodged at that same public-house, we could get what drink we liked at any time; so we drank and gambled every night; and thus our money was condemned every Saturday night. Of a Monday morning we hadn't a farthing left. Often on a Sunday, I can call to mind how we, and a lot of others, used to be locked up in a room upstairs, drinking and gaming. We were bound to be locked up, that so the churchwardens shouldn't find us out; and thus me and my *pals* were doing every Sunday. Yes; and I continued that course up to thirty-four years of age, when I married, knocking about from place to place, many days at a time walking with a hungry belly, looking for work, because I had got discharged through drunkenness."

"Did you ever sleep in the street?"

"No, I never spent a night in the streets, though I spent many a day; I always contrived to make shift to get a night's lodging somehow. I never lost my work for anything but drunkenness, for I could do my work well, and could earn twenty-four shillings a-week regular, if I had kept at it. All this while I never went to church. Until I joined your Society I had not been to church of a morning for thirty years."

"He did come once now and then to church at nights, after we came to live at Shrewsbury," added his wife.

"Yes, but how often was that? I might almost say I had never been to church but three times since I was seventeen. I went to church to be married, and to two of my children's christenings."

"Were you better for a while after your marriage?"

"Yes, for a little bit; but I lost work now and then through drinking—so that it was all the while moving from shop to shop; and the worst of it was I was getting fresh companions all the while, who did me no good. Then, when I was drunk, I was such a tyrant at home to my poor wife. I would take the poker and break up everything I came across. I remember some dishes and plates that belonged to my mother, worth fifteen shillings at least; I would not have parted with them when sober for five times their value. I took a poker one night, because my wife would not give me a shilling for drink. I thought she had got the rent-money by her, and I wanted a shilling of it, and it was all a mistake, she hadn't it at all; so I got a poker, and I took plate by plate, and broke up all the dishes and plates, which I valued for my poor mother's sake."

"He only did it because he was drunk, ma'am. He was always very good, and kind, and gentle when he was sober."

"Yes, it wasn't because I didn't love my wife and children, but because I was drunk. No man was ever fonder of his wife and children than I was when in my sober senses."

"He has forgot to tell you about Leicester, when he went on tramp there once, before we was married."

"Well, I went on tramp to Leicester at one time, and when working there the foreman used to encourage us men to have drink and dice in the work-room: the thing was this, the foreman was brother to the master, and they had a sister who kept a house for selling bread and cheese and ale—it was, in fact, a public-house; and so, every Saturday when our *log* [work] was taken, our wages would be so much, and our score so much, and sometimes our score was so heavy that we'd get nothing at all. There were fifty of us men working there. I almost lived on bread and cheese and beer then, bought off the landlady who was sister to our master. At last me and two more got discharged for disappointing a clergyman of his coat through drinking. I had scarcely a bit of shoe to my foot to go back to Birmingham, and I remember one of the men in the shop pulled off the slippers off his feet and gave them me. I had not a farthing of money. It took five weeks to tramp to Birmingham. We got work here and there on the road to help us on. I worked four days in Warwick. This was in 1841. It was in 1843 I married.

"I used to get twenty-four shillings a-week in general, but it was a wonder if I ever brought ten shillings home to my wife. I once left my wife and family, and went for work to Wolverhampton. Then I drank worse on Sundays than I ever did before. There was an order for mourning came in, the funeral was to be on Monday, and the master wanted all hands on Sunday; when he came into the shop to look after us we were all drunk—he found us all lying down, some on benches, some in the saw-dust on the floor, &c., &c. I had done my job, but the master wouldn't pay my wages—he withheld it because one of the men said he would summon him for not paying him the Saturday's money, and he thought that I should lend some of my money to the man for buying the summons, so he kept it back till that matter was ended. The man pledged his Wellington boots off his feet to get the summons. I wrote a very humble and penitent letter to my wife, for I had no money to send her."

"Ah, yes! that letter gave me great hopes of a change in him; it made me so thankful, I felt I could do without the money to get such a letter as that!"

"We came to Shrewsbury in 1845, and I became a teetotaller, but there was such jeering amongst the men, and no going to church on Sundays, no religion at all, that I gave it up after ten months; there was no one to sympathise with us, no one to lead us to God."

"Ah, our two lads became teetotallers when little ones, and we used to try to get my husband to read some of the temperance tracts, but to no purpose. He never would do so. So we thought of a new device: we used to wrap up his salt, when we sent his dinners, in a temperance paper or tract, and he would read that because he thought it was done by chance.

He read the 'Fool's Pence' in that way, and seemed much taken with it."

"Now I come to my worst drinking of all. Coming out of the public-house one day, my boy came and told me that his mother was taken ill in the yard. I knew what it was. She was confined. The child died. She had a narrow escape of her life then. I had been drinking nearly all that week, so that I had earned but four shillings that week, and out of that I had kept two shillings. Her illness made me *reflect in earnest*, though I was sodden in drink at the time; yet I went after that, and spent my boy's earnings, which he had saved for his mother. But I tried hard to be better, and for a month I went on tolerably; but it all came to nothing, and I went off again for a week's drinking. My poor wife then had a slight stroke. I was that ill on Sunday from the drinking that I could not stand. Then I made the resolution to myself not to taste any more, if possible, as long as I lived. I knew nothing of your Society then. Two months passed, and I kept firm. J. Clarke met me in the street, and invited me to join your Society, and told me he had been nearly six months in it. I came and joined: you were out that night for a week, and a navvy gave an address. Mr. Wightman presided. I began the very first Sunday attending church at nights; and attending your school-room meetings. It was your addresses there which first touched my heart, and by them

God convinced me of my sinfulness. No one ever came to see me, or reason with me when I was drinking; nor till after I had signed, and changed my way of life. I do believe, if clergymen wished to get a man out of drinking ways, they could do it, if they would but try. With *kindness*, you may do anything in the world with a man." [Here he burst into tears.]

"I used to swear awfully once. My eyes have got dim now; and it brings to my mind how I used to curse them. I was dreadful for that. I feel very different inwardly altogether. Sometimes I feel anger rise, and I check myself. I do not try in my own strength, but I get helped by God. He enables me to take things more coolly now. I don't let things put me out of the way as I used to do. I feel strength put into me — not my own strength — something different altogether. I have now been fifteen months in your Society. My course of living is altogether changed." [Here he again burst into tears, in which his wife and I joined.]

"There's not a Sunday that I don't go to church twice, and to your meetings afterwards. Last week I was overworked. On Saturday I worked from four A.M. till twelve P.M. I was too weak and ill to go to church, and never thought the staying away could have made me so unhappy as it did."

"I had to give him coffee on Saturday so many

times to keep him up to the mark ; he was near fainting at the last, and he was too tired when he got to bed to sit up to eat his supper. And he was too ill to go to church. But he would come to your meeting Sunday night."

"I came with an oppressed heart, and I went away with a light one."

Ah, my subject was "JESUS WEPT." What surer cure for a burdened heart than the sight of *the Man* Christ Jesus, our brother born for adversity. Dear John Ithell! After his week's hard work and close confinement, unable to attend for the first time since he had signed the pledge his parish church, God still had a message of love for him in the little room where prayer is wont to be made, and he went away comforted and blessed.

God be praised!

There are not three happier homes in England than those of John Ithell, Richard Daniels, and Tom Williams. It always does my heart good to call and have a chat with their wives.

The last time I was at Williams's house, they were at dinner. Fearing lest my presence should be an interruption at their meal, I proposed calling again, but the kind people would not hear of my leaving.

To prevent my feeling it an intrusion, a tumbler of pure water fresh from the pump was brought me,

and a delicious home-made bread-cake, on which I made an excellent luncheon whilst they dined.

Another man gave me the following account of himself lately:—

"I had been forty years drinking hard. The first time I went to your 'Reading' after signing the pledge, you said to us all, 'Dear friends, if there is any one here who has his load of sin still weighing as a heavy burden on his heart, come to Christ now—as you are.' So I thought to myself, that's meant for me. So I went home, and I knelt down all alone, and I said to Almighty God, 'I'm a great sinner, and I don't know how to come to Christ, I implore Thee to show me how to come, and I don't know how to change my way: oh! wash my sins away. Bring me to Jesus. Take me, as I am, wicked blasphemer as I've been, and drunkard. Change me, make me different.' And the Lord heard me, and pulled up my enmity as if by the root. And He kept me from scheming after the drink, for I used to scheme how to get drink, how to get an extra penny to spend on it, and how to get a drop given me; and the Lord kept me from cursing and swearing, too. I never could do that again, after all His mercy to such a sinner as me."

"Home, sweet home!"

"Be it ever so humble,
There's no place like *home.*"

CHAPTER IX.

"I HAVE cause to bless God that ever my husband joined your Society," said Mary Warburton a few days ago to me. "And when the neighbours call us Mrs. Wightman's saints and Mrs. Wightman's hypocrites, I wish there were many more such as we are, for we have as happy a home now as any one in England: bless the Lord for it!"

"Dear me!" said Mrs. Nicholl, "what a thing it used to be to prepare a meal for my husband! It was quite a puzzle what to do sometimes, he was so faddy. When I'd cook something very tasty for his breakfast, there was no knowing if he would touch it or not. The very sight of food used to turn his stomach. Now that he has joined your Society, he can eat anything. You would not credit it was the same man. He's got back to the taste of a child: he will come in to breakfast and take his butter-milk and bread with as much relish as either of the children; it goes down so sweet, and it does one good to see how he enjoys his food. He don't care what it is; he

is ready for anything, and it makes our meals so happy; he is so cheerful now; no grumbling as it used to be when he was drinking."

"I've cause to remember the 3rd of May," said Mrs. Davenport. "We couldn't have been lower anyhow than we were then. I went about everywhere as I could think of, to his old haunts, in search of my husband. Nobody had seen him, and at last he come in, and said, 'I've signed the pledge; remind me of it the first thing to-morrow, Mary, if I should forget it, for I mean to keep it.' And I said to him, 'Don't talk such nonsense, I don't believe you've done anything of the sort;' but he held to it; and he kneels down and prays, now, and is happy all the day long, and comes home so cheerful from his work. Oh, we have such peace and quiet! He never was noisy in his drink, but he would come in very drunk, late at nights, and lie down on the kitchen-floor, and ask for something to put under his head, and he would snore there for hours, and keep very still."

"I think Davenport will be a likely man for a missionary one of these days," said one of the men on whose judgment I could thoroughly rely. "He has never missed any means of grace since he joined us. And I had a sweet conversation with him at his own house the other day."

"How very wonderful! How little we thought it on the 3rd of May! do you remember his signing, and all the circumstances connected with it?"

"I do: but though he was so drunk, he was in earnest, and knew what he was about."

"Tell me where he has taken a house. I must go and see him and his wife surrounded by home comforts."

It was a sunny spot: the bright rays fell cheerfully through the windows into a clean, well-arranged kitchen. John Davenport was finishing dinner, and reading at snatches from the "Pilgrim's Progress." He looked up very brightly; the little child came in, and, running straight up to him, the father took him in his arms whilst his wife cleared the table. We talked about the past and the present, and they looked thoroughly happy. "I must kneel down and pray with you both, dear friends. Have you time, Mr. Davenport?"

"Oh, yes, ma'am, I should like you to pray with us. Our Scripture-reader came and prayed with us yesterday; he was so pleased to see we had got such a comfortable place."

And when we rose from our knees with full hearts, John Davenport said, "You'll come again soon, ma'am, I hope."

He added, seeing me admire the things in his room, "It's all teetotal furniture!"

"How delightful! But you have had hard work to get out of debt, I am sure?"

"We have paid every debt for the drink, I am thankful to say," said the wife, "and I don't think he will ever spend another halfpenny in drink as long as he lives."

"I hope not, ma'am, by the help of God!" His face looked radiant with happiness.

Willie Landon was a child of great promise, and no father could be prouder than Charles Landon was. "Though he's my own boy, I don't know a better lad anywhere; he is such a handy chap, I can trust him to do anything." He was only ten years old, the eldest of six. Playing on the banks of the Severn one hot summer's day, he was tempted to go in the river, with some other children, in a shallow spot. He took a chill, and died within a week. This was a trial, one to prove the Christianity of the parents. I never saw deeper grief. On Sunday, the day before the funeral, I went again to see them. Mrs. Landon was alone, sitting by her child's coffin, looking very pale. "It is such a comfort to see how my husband takes it." I thought of his former life, and the contrast between the *Christian* and the *drunkard* never struck me so forcibly. Mary had sympathy, love, and kindness now in her trial. Presently the children came in from school, and joined us upstairs, quiet as possible. I saw the father coming towards the house, accompanied by some near relations, they also joined us. I looked at Charles Landon—he is a man of few words and no culture, but for all that no one possesses more intense feeling. I saw the iron enter his soul as he gazed at the still face in the coffin. No one spoke. He broke the silence, "I can trust him to the Lord;" and then came an outburst of tears, showing that he spoke no words of mere cant. "Will you pray with us?" We all knelt, and we thanked God for all His mercies, and for the glorious hope of full redemption in Christ Jesus. I read "I am the Resurrection and the Life." We spoke of Jesus, and of the day of reunion with our lost ones, when God shall wipe away all tears, and there shall be no more sin, no more death. Next day I was with the bereaved parents at the funeral of dear Willie.

Contrast with this another working-man's home of which I know, where the mother was left to weep alone over her two dead babies, whilst her husband caroused at the public-house.

One Sunday afternoon Emma G. (who was staying with us) accompanied me on my rounds.

"Are there any sick for us to visit to-day?"

"Yes, there are two members. The one was at Bicton's Heath last Monday night, so he cannot be very ill, unless he took cold that night, which is very possible, for the people were assembled outside the cottage-door, and it was late and damp when we separated."

We went to another house on the way, where we found dear old Samuel Gough, poorly, and unable to be out. His heart seemed all right; he was resting on Jesus, and thought it "very long" since he had seen me. His wife was gone to the Bible-class held by the clergyman, or, when he was otherwise engaged, by his Scripture-reader.

She came in with a radiant face. "I've had such a beautiful meeting, ma'am! I have so enjoyed the class!"

After talking a few minutes on the subject which had occupied her, we went on to the two invalids whom we had set out to visit.

It is necessary to mention that these men were once as noisy and drunken as any in Shrewsbury. The contrast is so striking that every one who knows them is amazed at the change. The children used to be running about the streets on Sundays without shoes and stockings, ragged and dirty as possible.

We went first to Richard Greenwood. He had had a very sharp attack, which had confined him to his bed nearly a week. When we entered, we found him down-stairs, with his large Bible open, as if reading aloud. His wife and children were present.

The kitchen was scrupulously clean and neat, and the thorough appearance of a happy Sunday was the impression on entering the house. Everything was in its place, the hearth bright and clean.

"It wouldn't do to leave coming to Christ for a sick bed. You've told us so, and I'm sure of it."

"It is enough then to bear one's sickness, without having a burden of sin."

"Yes, indeed. If I had not come before, it would have been a poor hope for me when racked with pain. I couldn't have come then—I couldn't *think* at such a time."

"You had come heartily to Him before now."

"Yes, I had come, blessed be His name! and I had found peace. And He has been with me all through my sickness, keeping me looking to Him."

Much more was said. But it was the calm, deliberate manner, the settled peace on his countenance, the air of a man who means what he says, which struck me so much. The ground of his comfort could not be shaken, for he was resting on the finished work of Christ.

I said to him, "You are very weak yet."

"I am weak, but, bless the Lord! I want for nothing. I am glad to be down-stairs to-day, and when I can get out in the fresh air, I shall soon get up my strength."

At John Dean's we had a similar visit. The

kitchen was quite as neat and orderly. The whole family were assembled, except the eldest daughter, who entered whilst we were there. I thought we had never seen a sweeter sight on a Sunday afternoon than the air of calmness, peace, and rest in both homes. It was a scene to remember, and to bless God for. The little children looked so pretty, too, in their Sunday frocks, and well-polished shoes.

And there are hundreds of such homes now in Shrewsbury, from which the voice of prayer and praise goes forth, and where a good example is set by the head of the house.

When religion and total abstinence have entered as abiding guests, sanitary reform and civilization have begun their wonderful transformations. I notice invariably in such homes open windows, cleanliness, and comfort. Bad companions are wholly abandoned, and the family circle is the magnet of attraction to the working-man.

It would be well if the wife in every instance was a true helpmeet,—if she would so manage her household work that she could sit down with her husband as his companion and friend, when he returns home at night, with leisure to give him kind words, and to enter into his cares and trials. There are many such wives amongst our people; but there are some who are great hindrances, and who do not make their homes happy or comfortable.

It has been a great pleasure to me to see, not only necessary comforts purchased for wife, children, and home, but books, chimney-ornaments, pictures, and tasteful decorations finding their way also into the cottages. I feel grateful for possessing a quick eye for articles of vertù. Bronzed knights in armour, plaster cats and dogs of every imaginable colour and shape (who could have the heart to criticise ?), family photographs, china images, our family pledge-cards handsomely framed,—these are amongst the cherished household treasures in most of the changed homes.

I might fill volumes with happy home-pictures; the difficulty is which to select. I must add just two more: —

A bricklayer, whose wife was ill, asked me to visit her, and as it was more convenient for me to go in a morning, of course I always found her alone. She overwhelmed me with blessings every time I saw her. "I've cause to go on my knees for the change you've brought into my home. Never was anything more wonderful."

"The grace of God has done it, Mrs. Domville; your husband's heart has felt the love of Christ."

"It has; there's no hypocrisy about him; his gentleness, kindness, and patience, is past everything. He stopped four days from work last week to nurse me, and sat up night and day, and never left me; and oh, how he did pray to the Lord, by my side! When I think of all I've gone through during the years he drank, and how brutal he used to be, I can hardly credit that it is not all a dream, when I see how changed he is."

"Never speak to him about the past; let bygones be bygones."

"Oh, bless you, he's for ever speaking about it his self; there's no occasion for me to do so. He says, he can never do too much for me to make up for it all."

"Was his temper bad formerly?"

"Only when he was in drink, and he seldom came home sober; but when he was sober, never was there a sweeter temper; and now, when he comes home, let him be ever so tired, the first thing he thinks of is to go upstairs and bless the Lord, and pray to Him, and then he comes down looking so happy."

"If it was not for the drink, don't you think all our homes might be happy and bright?" said the daughter of a working-man one day to me.

One night we visited Mrs. Nicholls, whose husband, greatly reduced by drunkenness, had lately joined our ranks.

"It's up-hill work at present, ma'am," said Henry Nicholls, "so many debts to pay off; but I'm resolved to hold on!"

We spoke of others who had, by God's grace, recovered their position.

"Well, ma'am, we haven't to look far for instances of that; just look at John Newton! Why, there never was such a change in the world as in that house! There's ten children, all comfortable and well clothed; they was the most miserable set of half-starved, ragged creatures you ever seed. And as for the change in him that beats all! I declare if he ain't another man altogether! nothing puts him out of the road; and he does so pray night and morning. It looks as if his heart was changed."

"I'm sure of that," said Mrs. Nicholls, "she's been turned out into the street many a night when he was drinking; and now, nothing's too good to give her: she's got cause to go down on her knees to you for the change in her home."

"It was that made me sign the pledge. I thought if John can do without the drink, and he's the same trade as me, why shouldn't I try to do the same? The change in his home got over me, and he is so happy and cheerful."

"Do you see the reason, dear friends;—John Newton has come to Christ since he signed the pledge; and he attends church regularly, and has become a monthly communicant."

We talked a long time, and I felt, "What an influence *one* good example has!"

"The World on the Waters."

"Our ship is afloat, on the broad flowing wave,
And her proud pennant streams o'er the faithful and brave,
Our captain is Truth, and while manned by the free,
What crew,—nay, what men, are so happy as we?
Steady, boys, steady! and always be ready,
To rescue poor drunkards, again and again!"

CHAPTER X.

It is interesting, amongst the variety of characters in our Society, and the variety of occupations engaged in by the men, to find one who represents a large and too-often-forgotten class — the British seaman. Jack Thornvale is a fine specimen of that class; there is no man in our ranks possessed of more heartiness, good sense, and fervour in every good work entrusted to him by me. His past life on the sea, with its many temptations and trials, may not be uninteresting; and if it shall enlist the sympathies and prayers of any for a class too seldom remembered by us at the throne of grace, it will not be written in vain.

It may not be generally known that there are now missions to seamen.

" The field of their operation is among the fleets of British merchantmen and vessels of all nations in the various roadsteads and places of shelter for shipping; to seamen, pilots, trowmen, fishermen, lighthouse-keepers, and the inhabitants of the lesser islands, the Gospel is preached; and the opportunity is embraced of conveying to emigrants leaving their native land a parting word of Christian kindness—a word of counsel and of consolation. Nor is the work confined to British shipping; American, Prussian, Austrian, Swedish, Norwegian, Dutch, French, Portuguese, Spanish, Italian, Greek, and Russian vessels have been visited, and their seamen supplied with Testaments and tracts in their various languages. Roman Catholics on board Irish vessels have been visited also, and supplied constantly with tracts; and they have, in many instances, purchased Testaments.

"Within the last three years so rapid has been the progress of the missions, that sixteen stations have been added to the field of the old Bristol Channel Mission. The Society now occupies the best roadsteads of England and Ireland. In the Bristol Channel, off the Isle of Wight, off Plymouth, in Torbay, at the mouth of the Humber, and off Queenstown, may often be seen fleets of two hundred to three hundred merchant-vessels; and even five hundred to six hundred vessels may be counted at anchor when contrary winds prevail, while the Mersey is annually entered by many thousand sailors from all parts of the world. It may be stated as a gratifying fact, showing the interest felt in these missions, that the Government have kindly given permission for H.M.S. Calliope, lying at Plymouth, to be used for the purposes of the Mission."

"The World on the Waters" is the name of the little monthly penny book which gives an account of the operations of this Society; and most interesting are the journals thus published of the Scripture-readers and chaplains labouring amongst our gallant tars.

Jack Thornvale was apprenticed in Shrewsbury to a shoemaker. He ran away to Liverpool as a boy, and the charms of a sea-faring life seized hold of his young heart whilst roaming amongst the sailors in the docks. He there made acquaintance with the captain of a merchant-vessel, and engaged himself as an apprentice, to go a voyage on trial. He was afterwards legally bound for five years, and sailed to the West Indies, where, principally at Demerara, he got into drinking habits.

"There's great temptation in that West India trade. Every man was allowed a pint of rum a-day in our ship, which was enough to introduce any young man into the habit of drinking. I was in one of the head employs in Liverpool, where they were Quakers. Just about that time the teetotal cause began to make progress. It would have been a blessing for me if I would have abstained from drink from that time; I might have done well then; but because they gave coffee and cocoa instead of rum I was not content, so I left their employ and went into the East India trade, throwing up the chance of being captain in one of their vessels, for I was then second mate when I resigned. And now, just think, there are actually three of my fellow-apprentices at this moment captains of vessels in that same employ which I gave up."

"And what temptations to sin you might have escaped, too!"

"Yes, indeed, ma'am! mine has been a dear-bought experience. During the five years and half I was in the West India Islands, I've seen many a bright man lose his life through yellow-fever—the effects of drunkenness."

"How sad! Where did you go next?"

"I went into the North American trade for a little time. It was during the Canadian war. I there experienced one very remarkable thing. It was at Quebec. There was one of my shipmates got drunk on the shore, and he got drowned the same night; he was coming along the booms when he fell. The next morning I and another man were going on shore with a boat, and as we were coming to the booms we saw something in the water, which proved to be the body of our shipmate. His name was George White. Poor fellow! I remember we took the boat-hook out of the boat, and caught him by his clothes, and pulled him out. He had a bottle of rum in the breast of his shirt; and now, you'll hardly credit it, but we drank the whole contents, not giving it a thought that it had been the cause of his death. We then took the body on board; and as we were about to leave Quebec in two days, on that afternoon we took him on shore to bury him; almost the whole ship's crew went on shore, and all got drunk at the same place where our poor shipmate drank his last; and, what is more remarkable, from the same keg of rum which caused his death.

"That same night, the man who discovered the body with me joined me in purchasing the remains of that same fatal keg of rum; there were five gallons of rum, for which we sold our clothes. I had bought a pound of mustard, I recollect, and carried it in the breast of my shirt: this saved my life that night, I consider, as you shall hear. We took the keg of rum to the booms; but, when we got there, the boats were gone, so I left the man there in charge of the keg, whilst it was agreed that I, being the best swimmer, should make the best of my way to the vessel, which lay three quarters of a mile off, to fetch a boat. The mustard acted as a stimulant on the chest, and saved my life. It made my chest nearly raw though at the time. My mate had charged me to halloo out to him as I swam, that he might know if I was alive; but I didn't do this, and when I got back to him with the boat, I found him under the effects of the drink; he was lying with his head on the keg of rum, and would not give it up; he would not believe that I was Jack Thornvale, but would have it that I was the ghost of the shipmate we had just buried. All hands being drunk, it delayed us a day longer in Quebec. We went back to England then, and everything went on quietly till we got our wages on arriving in London, when I soon squandered mine."

"Did you never have a serious thought during all this time?"

"Yes, we had sometimes. I went to the cōast of Africa next voyage, in a small schooner called the Flora, fourteen good healthy men with me as ever you saw; and on our voyage out there I remember our *Sunday schooling* used to come over us sometimes, and we used to have such affecting scenes. Some of us had got copies of 'The Child's Companion,' and for all we were so wicked and thoughtless, we would read them through, and then we would pray that we might be different, for we felt we were not as we ought to be, and sometimes we would weep over the Bible; or when some one whom we respected was washed overboard, we would feel it much. But soon *drink* drowned every good thought and desire, and we got hardened, and forgot it all. This was a trading voyage to Gambia, where we purchased a deal of rum to trade with the natives. We left Gambia, and went 350 miles up the river. By having so much rum on board, we all took to drinking, and in less than fourteen days after only two of us were left alive, a young man belonging to the Isle of Wight, and myself; and thus we buried twelve of our bright men, as fine a set of young fellows as ever you saw; and a few hours after, when we went on shore again, we found they were all dug up by the wild beasts. This was not quite six weeks from the time of our starting in health, strength, and spirits from London."

"Oh, what sad recollections! If you had had a Scripture-reader or Chaplain on board, or some one who feared God, to teach and guide you, how different you might all have been! What did you do to replenish your crew?"

"At Gambia we engaged some Spaniards and Portuguese sailors to help us back to Falmouth. We then went to London, and came down to Liverpool by stage-coach (there was no railroad then), and I shipped in the Duke of Lancaster for Calcutta and China. This was a very pleasant 'out' till we got to the Cape of Good Hope, where we lost four of our men, who were washed off the jibboom. The way was this: six of us went to stove a jib, and four out of the six got washed overboard. It was dangerous work when it was stormy, and that Saturday night we knew it was a risk of life, for the wind was strong, and it blew a gale, and the helmsman was not the best, and we had a Saturday-night bottle of rum allowed us. I remember one of the four who perished saying, as he was going off with the rest to his work that night, "Well, George, don't let my grog get cold, it's ten to one if I shall ever return to drink it myself."

He said this as cool as possible; and he never did return. After that voyage, when I got back to Liverpool, I received 36*l.*, and spent it in nine days, and had nothing to show for it, not even a handkerchief, and I even forestalled 5*l.* of my next wages. The publican at whose house I spent it all gave me a bundle of pipes to take with me after I had spent all my money!"

"How you get robbed and cheated when drunk!"

"I went to Calcutta after this in the Dorothea, and left her to go to China in the opium trade. It was sickening to see the poor creatures who take to opium. It has such a stupifying effect; there! they do nothing in life but drink tea, smoke opium, and sleep! The Tartars live on rafts, and only go on shore on Wednesdays and Saturdays; no communication with them and the Chinese on the shore except twice a-week; but they might deal with the ships at any time. It was curious to see how they live; five or six whole families on rafts, with gardens as large as our churchyards floating on rafts! I got back to Liverpool by shipping in another vessel, and then went to Valparaiso, and there changed to a steamboat called the Peru. I stopped eighteen months in the steamer, and had at the rate of a double loon a-month [a loon is 3*l.* 12*s.* 4*d.*]; but all my money went in drink, so when I got to London I had to go off again to sea, and I went to the Brazils, and to

Ichaboe for guano; there I saw more drunkenness than I ever saw before in any part of the world; it was chiefly *brandy*. We had to get our guano there, and had to be supplied from other ships. I have drunk as much as four half-pints of brandy a-day there; and I saw fighting to a greater extent amongst the men than I ever saw before. I was mate of the Britannia of Liverpool, second mate of one of the seven vessels that first came to that island, so that I had an allotment of land given me as well as the others, and I gave it to the ship. On landing, you could hardly put your feet down on the ground for penguins, seals, and other amphibious animals, they were so thick, and the sea-gulls too. A 'mummy' was dug up from my allotment, the body of a Spaniard who died 1768. A water-cask and stave had been put as a mark on his grave. It went by the name of the Ichaboe mummy. It was dangerous work getting the guano, it is such a soft substance; and when undermined by digging it away, heavy falls of it would occur, which at one stroke smothered eight or nine men. The guano is seventy feet deep. We formed a graveyard at the back of the island, and in the course of nine months we buried forty men there. I came home to Bristol and Gloucester, and had then 123*l.* to receive, and I came to Shrewsbury for the 'show' and races; the money did not last me more than three months, so I was obliged to go to sea again."

"Well, really, I never heard such a history! Such a waste of life! Who would ever think it possible you could become a steady married man, A TEETOTALLER, and A CHRISTIAN!"

"Well, I had a strong detest of teetotalism then, I assure you, and the cause of it is worth naming; it may be a lesson to those who are only *pretending* to be teetotallers, and deceiving all the while. I was in company once with a man who called himself a teetotaller, and I was going into a public-house, and asked him to go in with me, when I called for rum. He asked for sixpennyworth of the same and a penny roll. And then he asked for a basin, and he deliberately broke up his roll, poured the rum over it, and when it was well soaked he ate it. I told him if that was the way he cheated the devil *I* would never be a teetotaller. So I judged of all the rest of the teetotallers by this man, which I own was not right. So I had a great detest against teetotalism altogether at that time; and during the time I was in Shrewsbury on that 'spree' I was with a lot of men in a certain public-house one day, and a teetotaller was in our company. We were all drinking together; he had his ginger-beer, and we had ale and rum. So there arose a strong argument along with the men and this teetotaller, and I laid a wager of five shillings that I would get him to break the pledge before he left our company. Now, the fact is, it served him right if I did get him to break it, because we considered that no teetotaller had any right to be in a public-house with such as we; it wasn't consistent or right of him; and I feel that I should deserve the same *now* if I were to go drinking ginger-beer or smoking with a lot of men who were drinking ale in a public-house. It's the *sort of company a teetotaller ought to give up.* Well, as they sat arguing with him about teetotalism, I went down-stairs and purchased half-a-dozen bottles of ginger-beer, and half-a-pint of gin, and me and the waiter put a little into each bottle, and I gave the waiter sixpence to bring these very half-dozen bottles which I had paid for; and she did so, and the teetotaller drank them all, and they made him *very drunk,* whilst *we* was pretty sober all the while, so I gained my wager. I tell this for teetotallers to learn a lesson not to associate with drinking men in public-houses, and thus to run into the way of temptation."

"But surely he *tasted* the gin, and *knew* he was getting tipsy."

"*He didn't take any notice of it,* but continued to drink on till he had finished the bottles, and then he was certainly drunk, and no mistake."

"Where did you go next?"

"To Bombay, in the Richard Cobden, belonging to Mr. Darby of Coalbrookdale, and had a *very* comfortable voyage. The captain was a Quaker, and the vessel a thorough teetotaller. That was the first teetotal vessel I ever stopped in for any length of time; I was eleven months in her. But so bent was I on being no teetotaller myself, that I was not content with continuing any longer, so I left that employ as soon as we came home. And I joined the Newfoundland trade, and we went on the Labrador coast trading, principally in seal-fish fishing, cod fishing, and fur trade; we used to find we did more with the natives through rum and tobacco than any other way. On the Labrador coast Indians live by hunting; trading vessels goes down there every summer from St. John's, Newfoundland. For some years longer I continued to go to sea from Liverpool, Bristol, and London. But I begun to get tired of it, and took it in my head I would rather settle on shore. I became a bit steadier, and then it was I picked up along with my present missus as is now, at Birkenhead, and I married her, and I must allow that I bless the day I ever did so. I only went a voyage or two to sea afterwards, as my wife was not contented to be left ashore at Birkenhead. I had several offers to take my wife to America, but she would not consent to leave England. An old captain of mine, in a situation for Mr. Darby at Saltney, obtained work for me on the Shrewsbury and Chester Line, and I came up to Shrewsbury with the first engine, by turnpike-road, drawn by horses. I found railway work quite as much a place for drink as seafaring business, and I must be the same as the rest of my shopmates, so that I drank very hard on times; but I am happy to say my family were never deprived of the necessaries of life through my drinking, as I was getting pretty good wages.

"This life went on for about seven years, when I went to Liverpool to see one of my shopmates off who was going to America, during the Crimean war. I went in a ship to the Great Britain, which was bound for Melbourne and Sydney, when the ruling passion came over me again; the old sensation was too strong for me; and I agreed with the captain to go with him at 6*l.* a-month, 3*l.* of which I agreed my wife should draw regularly. When I returned to Shrewsbury, and told my dear wife, she was very much cut up; I had three small children; it was no use vexing, as I had done the thing, so I gave notice to my master, and in four days I left my situation and went to Liverpool, my wife and children accompanying me to Liverpool to see me off. We got down off Holyhead, got foul of a wreck, sprung a leak in the stern by the fan, and had to put back to Liverpool. We were detained six weeks repairing, and so my wife and children came down to reside in Liverpool during that time. We at last got off and sailed for Melbourne, had a prosperous passage out, sixty-four days. We had the small-pox on board, and were twenty-two days in quarantine, then got product, and went from Melbourne, after discharging cargo and passengers, to Sydney."

"Did you lose any lives by the small-pox?"

"Not more than three. We came home to Liverpool in eighty-four days, left the vessel, came to Shrewsbury, had an offer to a situation at Hereford. I had then a tidy sum of money, and everything passed on very comfortable for a while. I began then to think of *sobriety*, and soon after your Society was formed in Shrewsbury for total abstinence; there had been one before, but I never felt induced to join it. I came to one of your meetings, and I was struck with the religious spirit in which you carried on the Society. So I took it in that light to become a member myself, as I saw the good effects done by it on other men. I have been a member now some time. I signed January 13th, 1859. It was the Gospel of Christ joined to the teëtotalism which struck me so much. Seeing, as I have done, the evils arising from drink, in every condition of life, I must say that I can hardly now consider a man who is not an abstainer to be a Christian—I mean I *cannot under-*

stand it—for THE DRINK LIES AT THE FOUNDATION OF ALL THE DEGRADATION AND SIN I HAVE EVER WITNESSED, and I trust I have done with it for ever."*

Here is a sample of the trials and risks our seamen incur. It is painful to think, out of the multitudes who leave our shores annually, full of buoyant life and spirits, how few comparatively return to England. It is impossible to hear Jack Thornvale's story without the conviction forcing itself on our minds that the mortality amongst seamen is almost wholly to be attributed to the use of ardent spirits. It is only one constitution in a hundred that could have stood it as my friend did.

"I don't believe any of the men who went those first early voyages with me are now alive. I believe they are all dead, except those few who took to total abstinence and continued in the service I left; and of these fellow-apprentices of mine, three of them are now captains of vessels in that same service."

Jack Thornvale is now an earnest Christian. He possesses good judgment, stability of purpose, and a loving, gentle spirit; qualities which make him very valuable to us, and render his home bright and sunny.

* Let the reader put himself into the position of degradation into which this man had ofttimes fallen through the drink, and he will not cavil at the conclusion to which he came. All depends on the point from which we view a subject.

O fellow Christians of England, let us offer special prayer for our seamen, and especially for the training colleges for the higher classes in the Navy.

It may be well to name some facts not generally known, which may be useful to any young lads inclined for sea-service from amongst our working-classes, showing the advantages to be derived by service in the Royal Navy.

The average *annual* wages are greater in the Navy than in the Merchant Service. The average of Merchant seamen earn only nine months' wages in the year. A man-of-war's man earns wages all the year round, even when sick or on leave; and good conduct or improving capacity advance him to higher ratings. There are also additional allowances in some ships, and promotion, gratuities, distinctions, and rewards for good conduct.

It is the *continuous service*, or *entry for ten years*, which offers such great inducement for entering the Navy, for there is no risk of disappointment, whilst it enables the seaman to embrace that branch of his profession which holds out the most advantages. "At the end of ten years' service, reckoning from eighteen instead of twenty years of age, as heretofore, the *Continuous Service Man* may, on discharge, receive a pension of sixpence a-day, or nine pounds four shillings per year; after fifteen years' service, a pension of eightpence a-day, or twelve pounds four shillings per year; and after twenty years' service, a pension of from tenpence to fourteenpence a-day (average one shilling), or eighteen pounds or nineteen pounds per year. Petty Officers and Leading Seamen's Pensions are proportionally greater; so that the man-of-war's man may, at the ages of twenty-eight, thirty-three, and thirty-eight, respectively, have earned a pension varying from nine pounds according to his rating; and if called to serve in the fleet, in the event of 'an armament or war,' *he will receive his pension in addition to his pay*, and he will enjoy this *for life*, being at the same time at liberty to earn what he can in the Merchant Service, or any other employment.

"The twenty years' service pension is certain, but the pensions for ten and fifteen years' service are granted at the discretion of the Admiralty; and as it is to be expected that, with the inducements now offered, the Navy shall never henceforth want volunteers, the opportunity will occur for maintaining a reserve of some thousands of these Short Service Pension men, well skilled in naval duties, under obligation to serve when called upon, should the necessity arise, but at liberty to follow their inclinations in other respects."

Hope for the Hopeless.

"Neither do I condemn thee. Go, and sin no more."

CHAPTER XI.

"I do believe, ma'am, there's some heart left in that girl."

"I am sure of it, Mrs. Langley, and by God's help we will yet rescue her from her life of degradation and misery."

So saying, I called at Mrs. Conway's, who kept a disreputable house, and looking up for a blessing, with a steadfast heart waited until my knock was answered by Charlotte herself coming to the door.

On seeing me she started, and would have withdrawn immediately, but I looked kindly and sorrowfully at her, and said, "I cannot speak to you here, Charlotte; will you come to our house at half-past seven to-night?"

She hid her face in her apron, and answered with a choked voice, "I'll come."

I waited till past eight that evening, and began to feel sick and sad, when I heard a gentle knock at the drawing-room door, and to my great comfort Charlotte stood before me.

"I couldn't come earlier;" and she turned away her face.

I took her hand, and placing a chair for her close to mine, I said, still holding her hand, "Charlotte, sit down by me. Don't be afraid of me. I am not going to say one unkind word,—not one word of reproach. I offer myself as a true and sincere friend to you,—as true a friend as I was to your poor father. You are now an orphan, Charlotte. If you will leave your present course of life, I will be like a mother to you as long as you live."

She burst into tears, and wept for minutes.

After a long silence, I added, "Dear Charlotte, this must be the turning-point in your life. I ask one thing—will you go into a penitentiary?"

"I will."

"God bless you, poor child! I do not ask you to enter ours, it would be too great a trial; but I will write to the Rev. ———, the chaplain of a penitentiary many miles distant, and see if I can get you admitted."

I spoke then long and fully of the sin of her past life, and of God's mercy in Christ, and having asked her to come daily to our house from morning till night, she went back again.

In the meantime I bought her a print gown, which she helped to make up for herself; for though very gaily dressed in the street, I found that nothing belonged to her; she was thoroughly destitute of clothing.

In a few days we started her off to ——, in company with a trustworthy person.

That day I could not rest—my heart was often lifted up in prayer for her. It seemed very wonderful, after so reckless and undisciplined a course of life, she should consent to enter a penitentiary; and I remembered that I had not said all I meant to have done about the *restrictions*, which might take her by surprise, and perhaps disgust her at first. So I wrote to her fully, strongly, and affectionately. I laid before her the past life she had led, and alluded to some facts connected with it which I had not touched upon in conversation, and then I implored her to confess all to God on her knees, and to ask Him to wash all her sins away, and to receive her as His child for Christ's sake. I ended with hearty promises of friendship, if she would be a good girl, and not disappoint me.

Never did a letter arrive more opportunely. Poor Charlotte, on arriving at the penitentiary, heard that her hair was to be cut, which I had forgotten to tell her. Of course she was in a terrible state of rebellion, and I believe she rather alarmed the authorities by her ill-behaviour, and her resolution to withstand this rule. She was, as might be expected, very impertinent, and was to be dismissed the house next day.

My letter turned the tide of affairs. She read it

and re-read it, and at last begged leave to stop one night longer, and even apologised for her conduct with sincere sorrow. And then, when bed-time came, she could not lie down; she was afraid to do so. Her heart was oppressed with guilt. The words in the letter spoke so plainly of her past sins. She was terrified at the amount of sin she had committed. Three times she tried to lie down and sleep, but each time terror came over her—the dread of all her guilt in the sight of God. At last, yielding to the earnest entreaty contained in the letter, that she would kneel down and confess her heart full of sin and sorrow to Him who alone could forgive sin or comfort her broken spirit, she did so. And as she knelt she wept, long and bitterly, tears of genuine repentance and sorrow. Words came to her relief, and she told God she was a lost sinner, and in broken accents she implored mercy and forgiveness. And she knelt on, she could not tell how long, praying, until she found pardon and peace.

She slept towards the morning, and awoke up refreshed and strengthened, with a softened heart; and like a little child in gentleness, she asked to be fully admitted, and patiently allowed her beautiful hair to be cut off.

More than fifteen months have passed, and dear Charlotte is continuing to give satisfaction. "Is not this a brand plucked from the burning?" I have been three times to see her, and to cheer her in her willing obedience. And I ask, "Will every one who reads this lift up an earnest prayer for a blessing on the young orphan girl?"

At one of the women's communicants' meetings connected with my Society, I asked those who were present one night, if they would undertake a new work for the love of Christ, and I named it as my wish that we should try to rescue some of our fallen sisters through their instrumentality.

The suggestion was received with much thankfulness and delight. I put down, accordingly, the names of a few married women belonging to my Society, to engage in this blessed work, and we agreed that they should first consult their husbands, and if they approved, we would meet together on the following Monday evening at the Vicarage for prayer.

The women did so, and came, according to appointment, on Monday night. After seeking God's blessing on their new undertaking, three of them expressed a wish to go that same night to reconnoitre the ground, and to form some idea of the work they would have to do.

To our great surprise, they returned in an hour, accompanied by two young women from the streets. We shall not easily forget the thankfulness and joy with which they brought these poor forlorn ones. My husband read the Bible and prayed with them.

His words of kindness and comfort touched their hearts, and they wept. Each had a happy and respectable home far away, from which she had come, beguiled by the cheap fares on SHOW MONDAY. *They fell that day;* shame kept them from returning home; they felt they could not face their parents, and thus they had continued a life they loathed, because they could not tell how to escape from it. The mention of their mother's fireside made them weep bitterly. They felt sure they would be received with kindness, if they could but get back. But they had no money. We gave them hot coffee, and bread and butter, finding they seemed in want of food. They were very grateful, and said several times, "We never had such kindness shown us before; we couldn't have believed it possible!" Within two days they were sent home, the one to Liverpool, the other to Wolverhampton.

From another young woman whom we sent to Liverpool the next week, I received the following letter:—

"DEAR FRIEND,—I reached home quite safe at a quarter to six on Tuesday evening, and my mother was very glad to see me. She told me, if I would promise to be a good girl, that there was a home for me yet; and I did promise that I would be so, and I will strive to do all that lies in my power for her, and to resist all temptations that lie before me. I shall go to a situation, as soon as I can get clothes sufficient. . . . . I return you my sincere thanks for your kindness in sending me once again to my happy home."

I refrain from entering further into particulars about this new and blessed agency in Shrewsbury, which is going on quietly and unobtrusively, yet surely and successfully, rescuing every week some precious soul from sin and degradation.

We ask for much prayer, and for an especial blessing on those self-denying women who, with family claims, do not think it too much to give a portion of their time *gratuitously* for the love of Christ, to bring their fallen sisters back to the paths of peace and virtue.

One day I half apologised to one of their husbands, because I knew his wife had been out on her mission of love until twelve o'clock the preceding night. "I hope, Mr. Johnson, you do not think I am encouraging your wife to neglect home duties?' "Oh, ma'am, don't say a word about that! it's nothing. If only one soul can be saved, is it not worth every effort? We are so thankful you ever thought of such a blessed work."

Such is the spirit in which this mission is being carried on. One night, on returning home late, I saw three of the husbands standing together in a public thoroughfare (the streets being perfectly quiet and empty), waiting to escort their wives home after their self-denying work. I thought, what a wonderful principle is the love of Christ!

I have occasionally accompanied one of my women by day to the places they visit, and without any hindrance have assembled some of these poor degraded ones to read the Bible and to speak to them. On one occasion, when ten of them were present, I asked each woman two questions,—"Have you a mother?" "Are you happy?" It was a sight to move a heart of stone; they wept as if their hearts would break, as they answered "No" to each question. They did, indeed, seem forlorn, without a home, a friend, a *mother*. I spoke of the penitentiary to them; but there were three things most revolting to their minds connected with the internal discipline of such asylums, which repelled any thought of seeking admission there,—1st. cutting off the hair; 2d. making it a rule that every inmate must stop two years before she is placed in service; 3d. locking up the probationers in solitary confinement for a month.

When we consider that very few, if any, enter a penitentiary with religious scruples about their past life, or godly sorrow for sin (and we need not be discouraged at this, for it is the religious teaching in the penitentiary which brings these happy results), how can we wonder that no undisciplined mind hardly will submit to conditions so humiliating and trying? To the cutting off the hair I especially allude,—that ornament which God has given to woman for a covering, and which is a symbol of modesty. A *real penitent* would, of course, submit to anything rather than go on in sin. But we are all *human;* why should there be added to the necessary restrictions of penitentiary life something at once unnatural and semi-barbarous, thus putting a stumbling-block where we ought rather to *allure* and win the prodigal to the Father's home? The haunts of vice are made attractive to entice victims. "The children of this world are verily wiser in their generation than the children of light!" We strangely forget His example who received His long-lost son with the welcome of a loving heart; for we see nothing to remind us of "the fatted calf, the ring, the joyous feast," in the outwardly strict and dull arrangements of a penitentiary. "We want something to remind us of *home,* a mother's love, and fireside," said one of these poor destitute women to me.

I am thankful to say we unanimously agreed to discard the three objectionable rules from our penitentiary at our next meeting, although, in justice to ourselves, it ought to be stated that we had greatly modified our practice for some time.

Our subsequent accession of numbers has shown us that we have not erred in so doing.

A policeman met me one night who has taken a great interest in our work amongst this class. He said, "You have begun at the right end by striking at *the drink*, for that is at the bottom of more than half the sin and sorrow of our streets." And he added, "I have seen so much of that unhappy class of women, and I may venture to speak upon the subject, because my experience may be useful to you. If you will go on as you have begun amongst them, you may rescue most of them from their bad ways. Poor things! there's many a heavy heart amongst them; indeed, there's scarcely one but what loathes the life she leads, and would thankfully give it up, if she knew how; they know nothing but sorrow and bad treatment; what they want is a place that shall be like a *home*, to restore the feelings they have lost, where they shall be treated kindly by one who will act like a mother towards them. That's what our penitentiaries ought to be; just such *homes*, where they ought never to be locked up. That locking-up system shows a sad want of knowledge of character; it's all wrong. When you want to restore confidence and to build up character, you should *trust* a person, and treat them kindly, and then no one would ever need to send for a policeman into a penitentiary, as I was once sent for into one, to quell a row. Why, there should be no such thing known in a penitentiary. If *love* ruled it couldn't be so; there would be order and peace there!"

These are valuable remarks, coming from such a quarter. They reminded me of Charlotte's words the first time I saw her at the penitentiary at ——, after she had finished her solitary term of probation, and was in full work amongst the other inmates. "Oh, ma'am, we have such a good matron! quite a mother to us all. I couldn't bear to grieve her, she is so good to us; she is very firm, too, for when she says a thing, she means it; but we see she loves us, and cares for us. And I can't help loving her, it's just as if she was our own mother."

We have learned some valuable lessons from the testimony of our fallen sisters. I will put it in their own words, which are most touching:—

"You could not do better than strike at *the drink*. You have began at the right end there, for that is at the root of all our sin and sorrow."

"Except for *the drink*, I should never have *begun* this life. And we could *none of us continue* it except for that."

"We are obliged to drink before we go out."

"When we are in our sober senses you would pity us. We could tell you such a tale of sorrow. No one cares for us. Even those who are as bad as ourselves point at us."

"Except for *the drink*, we could not dare to show our faces in Mardol" (the name of a street). "We could not, if you would give us the whole of Shrewsbury."

We have often deplored the fact that few persons ask for admission into penitentiaries, except those who are utterly destitute, or else broken down in health. In fact, they seldom come unless they can go nowhere else, as a kind of last resource.

This is probably the reason more good is not effected. Many of the inmates are so incapacitated in constitution, it is almost hopeless for them to be able to earn their bread when they leave the institution.

By our new agency we have gained access to a better class, at an earlier stage of sin, before the constitution is enfeebled, or the heart seared. Some who have only just commenced a life of sin have been rescued, and who, except for the love which would take no denial in obedience to the command, "Go ye into the streets and lanes, and compel them to come in," might have been left to perish, as too many of their unhappy sisters have done.

Our Penitentiary is nearly full. There is only room to add one more inmate. We have been told, upon the best medical authority, that the present building is in too confined a situation to ensure the health of the inmates.

We have no space for out-door exercise, nor for drying the clothes on washing-days.

There is also no laundry belonging to the house; the only room which can be appropriated for that purpose is in the middle of the house, consequently the stove arrangements necessary for drying the clothes render the building still more close and unhealthy.

But what are we to do without funds?

We are in want of money to enable the Committee to rent premises which are suitable. We want a place, beyond the precincts of the town, where we could ensure plenty of fresh air, water, and space for out-door exercise and drying ground.

Shall we be straitened for want of funds? Will not Shropshire answer our appeal, and enable us to carry on the good work with more prospect of success than we have yet had?

We rest our case in His hand who says, "The silver and the gold are mine," and earnestly pray that He will open the hearts of His people to help us in our work of love and mercy.

Safely Landed.

"They wear the crown of life on high,
They bear the shining palm,
Where angels 'Holy, holy,' cry,
They join the glorious psalm.
But we poor pilgrims journey on,
Through this dark land of woe,
Until we go where they are gone,
And all their joy shall know."

CHAPTER XII.

"How many have you lost from your number by death?" asked a friend one day.

"We have lost five. You will see all about dear Stedman's death, and John Davies', in 'Haste to the Rescue,' but there are three more to add now."

"Have you a good hope of those three?"

"Yes, blessed be God, we have."

John Jones was discharged from the army, sick and unfit for service, after the troops returned from the Crimea. He was lodging at Tudor's, in Bythell's Passage, when I first saw him. His pension had ceased, and at his request I wrote to a friend to get it renewed, if such a thing was possible. Having failed, we looked after him; but it was too late, "the want had gone through him," and disease had made inroads upon a constitution already greatly enfeebled by the privations and trials in the Crimea.

"I was as strong a young fellow as ever left England to go to war," said he one day, as I sat talking to him. He regularly attended our school-room meetings as long as he was able, and joined our

Society; as he never touched drink, he had nothing to give up. He had seen the bad effects of it in the army, and loathed the sight of it. I found, on conversation with him, that he was brought to Christ whilst in the Crimea. He spoke ot Captain Hedley Vicars with affectionate regard, though he did not know much of him.

He was many months in the Infirmary, during which time I visited him; but, knowing that he was well looked after by the chaplain, I did not go very often.

He dined every day in our kitchen, upon becoming out-patient; and then suddenly changed his lodgings to the Abbey Foregate, on account of the militia being called out; after which he never came again to our house, because of the distance after the fatigue of parades.

I heard very soon after that he had become worse in health, and had returned to the Infirmary. I was just going to see him when, to my dismay, I found he had died the day before, at the place where he lodged. He was buried with military honours, the expense being taken by the captain and militia-men.

It was a great grief to me that I never saw him again. Many a sweet conversation have we had together, and often his faith and love refreshed me. Sometimes, when downcast, "How shall I ever have strength to earn my bread?" rose to his lips, and I comforted him by reminding him of God's love and mercy; and once I said to him, "Oh, John, do you want to walk by sight instead of by faith? I will promise that you shall never want, but when you leave the Infirmary, I will look after you as if you were my brother!"

This brought the tears to his eyes. "I have no right to expect this kindness."

"Would you not do the same for me, if you were able, and I was a poor brother or sister?"

"Yes, I should count it an honour."

"And so do I count it an honour to help any child of God in your condition, so don't be faithless, but trust in Him. You shall never want, so long as I can help you."

"But I don't like to burden any one."

"We cannot always do as we like. You must not be proud, my dear friend. God has taken away your power to work, and it gives me pleasure to help you."

Very few of our members knew John Jones; he was a stranger in Shrewsbury, and he was so long in the Infirmary out of their sight. When I heard of his death, I felt he was taken from sorrow, sickness, weariness, and penury, to be with Jesus. He was cared for to the last, I heard, though I knew not of his illness till too late; and it was comforting to think of his funeral being so amply provided.

Thus God never suffered him to want.

N

The next who died in our ranks was a Welshman named John Williams, who had belonged for some years to a Total Abstinence Society, called the "Rechabites." He joined us, and in the course of a few months a marked change came over his spirit and tone of mind.

He took special delight in our Saturday-night prayer-meetings, and was generally present, taking part himself. There was something very humble, earnest, and real in his supplications.

One Saturday night he was pleading with his usual fervour in prayer, and we remembered his saying very earnestly, in his touching Welsh accent, "Lord, keep us ever looking to Thee—keep us ever close to Thee—close to Thy bleeding side. Lord, Thou knowest our hearts, keep us from sin; wash us all, gracious Father, in the blood of Christ." . . .

He did not seem ill that night, but some remarked afterwards that he looked very wan and haggard. But he was getting old, and I only noticed that his prayer was very solemn and earnest that night.

On the following Saturday he sent a message by one of his fellow-workmen, asking our prayers.

"I don't think he'll get over it, somehow; he looks very bad."

I went to see him, and found him suffering from jaundice and inflammation of the lungs. He was quite calm and sensible, and followed me in prayer as

I bent closely over him. The foreman came to see him whilst I was with him and his wife, and bending over him, asked him, in a gentle voice, "Well, John, how are you? are you able to rest on the Lord Jesus?"

"Yes," said the dying man, "I can."

"Bless the Lord for it! You can look to Him without fear?"

"Yes."

It was good to hear the questions asked, and answered thus.

He died Monday evening, about an hour after my last visit. Could we have any doubt of him?

Henry Blent signed the pledge, July 31st, 1859.

He was then the prop and support of his mother, old Mr. Blent having long become helpless from paralysis.

They were chairmakers, and lived on St. John's Hill. They left for a cheaper house, and I lost sight of Henry for some time, and then heard he was ill. He was ten months in consumption, gradually fading away. During that time he was regularly seen by me, and for the last few months I hardly missed a day.

He had outgrown his strength, and measured six feet two inches; he was twenty-one years and five months old when he died. I did not take any notes of my visits, being so fully occupied. He was very gentle and patient, and knew he should never recover. One day, towards the close of his illness, when he was suffering greatly from his breathing, and was too weak to sit up in his bed, suddenly, during a little silence, as I was kneeling by his bedside, his countenance lighted up with wonderful joy, and he looked glorious. "Dear Henry, what thought passed over your mind this moment?"

"I was thinking of that city which hath foundations, whose builder and maker is God."

"What made you think of it?"

"Mr. Powell was reading about it to-day. Oh! I shall soon be there, *and see* JESUS!"

One day I asked him to send a message by me to the Meeting,—"A message from a death-bed will be remembered."

He was too weary and ill, and languidly shook his head. His chest was so oppressed he could not speak even in a whisper, the cough was so bad. Next day (Sunday), after praying with him, I was leaving the room, when he called out, "Oh, stop, I have a message."

Not thinking of my wish of the preceding evening, I imagined he was going to give me a message for some one down-stairs.

"Tell them at your meeting to-night" (and he spoke so deliberately), "tell them that Jesus is a firm Rock, and a sure Foundation. I have found Him so.

Tell them to come to Him; He is the only Saviour. Tell them to look to Him; He will keep them close to Himself. Oh, if I had not found Him before I was ill, where should I have been now?" Here he threw up his arms, and with a look of anguish at the bare possibility of such a state, he shook his head, as if to say, "I should have been lost." The look and gesture were most significant and solemn. He proceeded, after a pause, "Tell them I have found Him in my presence; He has known all my wants, and has supplied them. I have never wanted anything and asked for it, but I have had it."

What a sweet testimony from a dying bed! I had conversed so much and closely with him that I knew he was resting on the Rock of Ages. This was, nevertheless, inexpressibly precious to me, for the sake of others, and I shall not easily forget how it solemnized every countenance when I read it that night at the close of our Meeting. I was afraid of trusting my memory; I therefore took down Henry's words in pencil, that I should not alter them in any way, but give the message as I received it from him.

One day, when I came to his bedside, he said, "Stoop down, I want to tell you something." I knelt by him, "Look here at these strawberries,—are they not beautiful? I was longing for some, my mouth was so dry, and I asked God to send me some, and I thought every minute you would come in, and bring me some, but you didn't come; and then Mr. Powell came in, and he said, 'Henry, can you eat some strawberries? for I have brought you some.' Wasn't that wonderful?"

He added, "I have never asked for anything yet but He has given it me!" .

"Did you ever ask for restored health?"

"No, I left that to Him. He knows best."

It was a very trying scene, the extreme weakness and emaciation, with the bones coming through the skin in many places. But we never heard him complain. One leg swelled at last.

"My poor leg! I do pity it, poor thing! See how it is swelled! it is very bad; will you rub it?" And then when I began to do so gently, he said, "Did I seem to complain? He is very merciful to me. Oh! it would be very wicked to complain, but I can't help but pity my leg, poor thing! Isn't it very bad?"

There were those in our Society who kindly sat up with dear Henry. Gentle and kind women, who were willing to help his poor mother and sister by relieving them occasionally of this burden.

One evening he was very downcast. With difficulty I gathered from him that he was fretting about the expense his funeral would be to his afflicted mother. "Rest your heart about that, dear Henry. There are some of us who would think it a privilege to undertake the last kind office for any child of God:

and so I promise you we will manage it all very nicely."

A load seemed taken off his mind.

At last God answered our prayers, and called Henry Blent to his rest.

I chose the spot of ground for him near Stedman's grave. And a lady who had kindly visited him and ministered to his wants helped in sharing the expense of his funeral.

Six of the members acted as bearers. It was one of the most thoroughly wet days we had this rainy summer. None of the females of his family attended, nor could I.

Upward and Onward.

"Let us lay aside every weight, and the sin which doth so easily beset us, and let us run with patience the race that is set before us, LOOKING UNTO JESUS."

CHAPTER XIII.

It was a lovely autumnal night; the moon was up, the air was calm, and peculiarly refreshing. Mary G——, who was staying with us, begged to accompany me on my night rounds. We started at half-past six for one of the suburban districts, my honest friend, Jack Thornvale, acting as escort. I had snatches of conversation with him between the visits we paid, which will not be forgotten through eternity. He spoke of himself, and the grace of God, and Christ's love.

"I am glad to hear you make one observation at our meetings,—you often say it, but I don't think you can say it too often."

"What do you refer to?"

"That, if it were not for the eternal results, you do not think you could have had courage to have begun or carried on such a work amongst us; that you wouldn't care for teetotalising us, if it was not for the bearing it has upon eternity; that you only care to bring us to Christ; and that is why you never speak a word to us about temperance or drunkenness after we have signed the pledge: you only speak of Christ, and our need of Him."

"I am so glad to hear you say this. People will keep telling me, that if our meetings are so exclusively religious and devotional, I shall drive away the members."

"If they had been temperance meetings, I don't think that I should have kept on as I have. It is the comfort we get by having Christ set forth to us so constantly that keeps us together,—it's wonderful to see how one after another becomes changed men."

"It is, indeed."

And then I thought of some, whom nobody would have dreamed of ever seeing otherwise than random, worldly characters, when the drunkenness was given up, who had become gentle, loving, earnest Christians.

Oh, how precious to me is the *intelligent Christianity* of many in our ranks! Such a contrast to some who have been habitual attendants at church, as a matter of course, all their lives, and who listen with unimpassioned heart to the most solemn warnings and the most earnest appeals, and can no more give an answer to the question, "What must I do to be saved?" than the heathen.

I have listened to the religious experience and confessions of some of our members with perfect amazement. The deep teaching of God's Holy Spirit has done wonders amongst them. Coming to Christ as lost sinners, with nothing in their hands,—their very teetotalism being a brand and a mark of scorn in the eyes of the Pharisees (a very large sect in every age)—they have earnestly sought, and have found, peace, and joy has followed. There is hardly a *doubter* amongst them. Instead of looking within, and watching their own frames and feelings, and doubting whether God can love them, they have so loathed self, that they have thankfully turned to look off unto Jesus alone; and thus, before they were aware of it themselves, like Moses, "who wist not that the skin of his face shone," they have reflected Christ's image in their lives and conversation. These simple-hearted, true disciples have multiplied amongst us, unknown and unnoticed. But Jehovah has hearkened, and heard it, and a book of remembrance has registered their names. "And they shall be mine, saith the Lord, in that day when I make up my jewels."

It was on August 24th, 1858, that we met, for the first time, in St. Alkmond's school-room, for our "Readings," at the earnest entreaty of the people. "Indeed, ma'am, we shall soon spoil your carpet; we are not fit to come in with our dirty shoes,—such a lot of us." Eternity alone shall unfold the result of these meetings. We have seen wonderful things take place there. Sometimes, when our Society (in the early days of our work) was occasionally convulsed within by some jealousy, heart-burning, or mutual misapprehension of character, I have seen, at the close of our meeting, the chafed spirit calmed and comforted, the angry look has given place to one of gentleness and kindness, ungenerous suspicions have been flung away, and men have joined in conversation like brothers who had entered the room as foes.

I attach great importance to these *religious* meetings, especially on a week night, as a help upward and onward.

It may be well in breaking new ground, and to arouse public attention to the claims of total abstinence, to have lectures to inform the uninstructed on the evils arising from intemperance, and to show the benefits of abstaining from "the drink." But for those who have signed the pledge, temperance meetings seem to me quite unnecessary. We have never had them, and yet our numbers increase, so that we now number upwards of four hundred and fifty men, two hundred women, and four hundred juveniles.

I am more than ever convinced that there is very little to be gained by giving to the working classes lectures of an exclusively secular character. The people are, for the most part, too wearied with the daily struggles, cares, and anxieties of life, to listen to anything which is foreign to their own case, and in which they have no interest. The fact is, we have too long erred in withholding our *sympathy* from them, and in not speaking to their hearts. We have not cared for the burdens which press heavily on them, the sorrows which need to be soothed, the hearts which yearn to be comforted. We have given patronage and condescension, in the place of seeking *their friendship*, and thus we have failed to get their hearts. We have not placed before them a *motive* strong enough to make the hard battle of life a matter of interest and enjoyment.

Dull religious exhortations disgust and weary. It is not *religion*, but a loving, living, sympathising *Friend*, that the people need. They want a SAVIOUR, the risen, exalted, loving, ever-present Saviour who died for them; the *Man* Christ Jesus. Nothing short of *the Gospel* will ever meet the need of human hearts. And if any people especially need "the tidings of great joy," and do receive it gladly, it is emphatically the working classes.

Amongst the special scenes in our school-room I must not forget last New-year's Eve. At the request of the people I met them there at half-past ten o'clock, Saturday night, December 31st, 1859. It was touching to hear them say, "We have for so many years drank out the Old Year, and we have made it a season of blasphemy and drunkenness. Let us meet together to ask God's blessing upon us. Will you meet us for prayer and praise?"

With great joy and thankfulness I did so. The

room was thronged. After our opening hymn, prayer, and Scripture, I called upon three men to offer prayer. We then sang a second hymn. We went on thus, singing between each third prayer until ten minutes to twelve, when I proposed that we should continue kneeling, and each pray in silence until midnight. When the church clocks had struck the hour, we rose from our knees and opened the New Year with a hymn of praise. It was most thrilling—the solemnity, the perfect order, especially the ten minutes' deep silence, which was only broken by a gentle, unconscious sigh, now and then, from some earnest worshipper. The fervour and humility of those prayers will never be forgotten. No one was passed over in the supplications, from the Queen to the peasant. Our army, navy, and sailors, our training institutions for the same, all the ministers of God's holy Word and Sacraments, the missionaries at home and abroad, Scripture-readers, Sunday-school teachers, and children, all were remembered.* The Spirit of God was present to bless. And it was remarkable how calm and happy each face looked, as I stood at the door to shake hands with every member, and to present them with a card containing our new-year's motto. It was beautiful to see the order in which the assembly broke up.

* Except God's ancient people Israel, whom we have especially remembered since, to make up for our omission that night.

The following evening, at the close of our usual "Reading," I told the people that the sweet savour of their prayer-meeting still rested on my heart, and that I had never spent a happier evening; adding, "Could we not have a similar meeting *quarterly?*" The men surrounded me before I left the room, and begged me to reconsider my proposition: "Would it not be better far to have it *monthly?*"

The next morning one of the men was sent to me with a message from fifty others, suggesting that we should fix on the Saturday night before our monthly communion for the prayer-meeting. We therefore carried out their wishes, arranging to meet at eight o'clock instead of half-past ten, and to make it one hour long. My husband said to me, "You must hardly expect such a meeting as you had on New-year's Eve; the solemnity of the season had something to do with the impressive effect."

However, our first monthly prayer-meeting was quite as delightful as the other had been. In some respects it was more so. And at its close the dear people implored me to meet them *weekly*, saying, "Saturday nights have been our principal drinking time, being pay-night, and they are times of great temptation to us all. Oh, do let us meet together *every* Saturday night; it will give us such a *lift* for our Sundays!"

From that time we have never missed these prayer-meetings; to me they are the sweetest in the week, and often when wearied in mind and body I have felt the soothing influence of the prayers so simply and fervently offered. A marked growth in grace has followed, and many who have been present will remember through eternity with grateful recollections their own prayer-meetings in our school-room.

A few members had met long before this, at 7 A.M. every Sunday for prayer and praise, in St. Michael's vestry, by the kind permission of the Incumbent. At the request of the people this meeting was now transferred to our school-room, when the numbers speedily increased to sixty. It is so refreshing to hear their hymns from our house at this early meeting. I do not feel equal to attending personally, only twice having been up in time to do so.

Several cottage prayer-meetings have also sprung up amongst the members in different parts of the town during the last twelve months, the mellowing effects of which have been felt and seen in those who have regularly attended them.

One night some working men were in our dining-room, and we fell into conversation, which is given here as a sample of the interest with which religious subjects are entered into. Henry Webster, who had then been six weeks in our ranks, and had never missed attending church and the meetings, was speaking of the change in his feelings towards God.

"I never could have credited there was such

enjoyment to be found in religion. The more I go to church, the more I want to go. I can't hear enough to satisfy me. I want to learn more all the while. Religion is a thing not to be acquired all in a moment; one must come at it gradually. When Jesus cured the blind man, He did not do it all at once; He first made the clay and anointed the eyes: and the man did not see all at once, it was only a glimmer at first."

Percy Granville, who was sitting next to him, observed, with a smile, "My dear friend, read the 16th of Acts, the account of the conversion of the jailor. There's no degrees in salvation. He asked, 'What must I do to be saved?' and was told, 'Believe on the Lord Jesus Christ and thou shalt be saved;' and he was a saved man at once, and rejoiced the same hour."

"That's true," said Henry; "and the man who was lying at the pool of Siloam, and had lain there a good longful time, because no one would help him to step in, so that a great many were cured before him, as soon as Jesus saw him, and spoke the healing word, he was cured at once, and took up his bed and walked. But it is not always so. Some have to be healed by degrees."

"It is according to our faith," observed Percy. I interposed with the observation that knowledge and sanctification admit of degrees—that we do not all at once apprehend what *sin* means, we see some open heinous acts at first— but we have to learn gradually by experience that our NATURE is utterly corrupt and sinful, and that unless the Holy Spirit by His mighty grasp hold it in abeyance, it will rise up into sinful actings, and bring forth evil fruit. "The enemies of Christ, not understanding this," I added, "expect the believer to be without sin, and so they watch him, and expose every fault, be it of temper or anything else, and pronounce him a hypocrite. But God sees the struggle within, and the deep anguish after every fall, and He knows the sincerity of heart. David is an instance of this. No doubt the ungodly in his day thought him a terrible hypocrite, and spoke of his sins in proof of it; but the Holy Spirit calls him 'the man after God's own heart.' It shows the necessity of keeping close to Jesus, or else we are sure to fall, and then the enemies of God take occasion to blaspheme."

"No man ever repented so much as David did," said Henry Webster.

Here old Davidson, who had been a silent listener, added his word, that he did not quite agree with that; he thought others repented quite as much, without any one knowing it.

"Repentance, dear friends," I remarked, "means not only sorrow for sin, but a change of mind, and turning from it. For instance, if either of you intended to go to Frankwell, and found out that you were on the road to Meole, you would stop, turn back, and not rest until you got into the right direction."

"Yes," said Percy. "Repentance means not only sorrow for sin, but turning back from it, hating it, and watching against falling into the same sin again."

This conversation is recorded exactly as it occurred, and shows the intelligent interest taken in religious subjects.

Early in the spring I received a letter from a personal stranger, the Rector of ——, in a neighbouring county, who, having read "Haste to the Rescue," wished to begin a similar work amongst his people. He wrote to ask me to send him a man from our ranks who was fit to be a Scripture Reader, and who would work for Christ amongst a hitherto inaccessible people in his parish, who were very much given to drink. There were three men whom I could safely recommend. One of these was a carpenter, who worked at his trade thirty miles from Shrewsbury, returning home only on Saturday evenings. His former history is striking. One Saturday he was waiting with his fellows for his wages at the public-house where they were paid, when John asked for pen and ink. Drawing a piece of paper from his waistcoat-pocket, he wrote on it a form of pledge against all intoxicating drink, and signing it first himself, he handed it to the other men to do the same. Some laughed, but two men signed it. At that time he knew nothing about our society. It was shortly after this his wife came to one of our Tuesday-night readings, whilst her husband was from home. She told him about it, and the next Sunday he accompanied her, and thus they both joined our society. From that time John became a more thoughtful man. He had been brought to the knowledge of the truth through his wife; but he grew in grace, and as the clergyman's wife in the village where he lodged during the week had begun a similar work to ours, he became her chief pioneer and helper. I felt very sorry to remove him from so useful a sphere of labour. But Mr. C—— thought John the very man for the post, his previous work having prepared him for it. When I mentioned it to him and his wife, they at once acquiesced, saying, "It will be a blessed thing to have nothing else to do but to win souls for Christ." John gave notice to his master immediately, and was ready in a week to take his family to R——. Five months have passed, during which a most interesting correspondence has been kept up between us; and his Rector has from time to time corroborated John's statements, and speaks in the highest terms of him and his excellent wife. Weekly cottage-readings, prayer-meetings, and a course of daily visiting, carried on in a spirit of humble dependence on God, and with a single eye to His glory, are bringing forth blessed results.

In one of Mr. C——'s letters he writes: "I have every reason to be perfectly satisfied with John's proceedings. The man's religious principles are more and more developing themselves. I am much pleased with the sound Christian views which he manifests, both on the temperance question and on other points. In fact, he and his wife are a great comfort to us. I have just now left home for a few days, which I do with much greater satisfaction, knowing that I have two in the parish who are taking a lively interest in the souls of the people. . . . There is considerable stir amongst us on the temperance question, and several, both adults and young persons, have signed."

It is cheering to read in John's letters, "I pray earnestly to God to give me courage and strength to go on boldly with the work. I meet with some cases that give me great encouragement, and others that cast me down, which I must expect; I will sow the seed by the help of God, and He will make it bud and bring forth fruit. My master gives me great encouragement to go on with the work." Again he writes, "I believe there is good going on. I have seen the tear wiped away in several instances, which is not a bad sign; I pray earnestly for the Holy Spirit to help me, and for strong faith in our Lord and Saviour to enable me to perform the very important duties that are appointed for me. I always remember you and Mrs. L—— and the societies which belong to you at the throne of grace."

About four months after John —— left Shrewsbury, a stonemason belonging to our ranks went to Chester, owing to a strike in the yard in which he worked. He wrote to me from thence, "For the last nine or ten months I have felt a strong desire to be working entirely for Christ. I often thought of speaking to you about it before I left Shrewsbury; but since I came here something seems to be telling me I must write to you. The way I should like to work for my Saviour is to go for a missionary to the poor heathen, to tell them about Jesus. That is the way that seems uppermost in my mind. I should like to be working for the Lord entirely." He added, "Many poor men like myself have gone to tell about Jesus through the help of a gentleman or lady."

I wrote to advise him to wait—and to pray. That he might work for the Lord as fully in his occupation as if he were a missionary—that we had so many thousands of *home* heathen close to our doors—that it would require much time and training for an educated man to learn a new language, how could *he* manage it? &c. Why not, if an opening occurred, take such a situation as our friend and brother John —— had done, in an English parish?

Several letters passed between us. In one of his he wrote, "I have thought much and prayed much for the Lord's guidance. I see it would take too much time to get prepared to go abroad, and many souls might be saved during that time. I firmly believe it is the Lord's will I should be wholly engaged in working for Him. My desire is to work for the Lord in the way that shall bring the most souls to Jesus. The only thing I feel worth living for in this world is to live a child of God. Before I was converted, my desire was to learn as much as I could about earthly things, but now I only care to learn about heavenly things. My desire increases to work for Jesus; I should take so much delight to fetch in fellow-sinners and to tell them of Jesus." Again he wrote, "Oh! the desire that burns within my soul to begin. I pray very much about it, and I believe the Lord will direct me aright."

Our friend, the Rev. J. ——, came in unexpectedly to breakfast one morning, in his way home from Ireland, when one of the letters from Edward had arrived. I spoke of him, and to my great joy Mr. —— offered to take him for one year as Scripture-reader in his own parish. Thus was the way most unexpectedly opened for the commencement of a course consecrated wholly to God's service. It is too recent to relate any results. May I ask for the prayers of all who read these pages for the two men who are thus working at a distance from us in the Lord's vineyard?

It is not to be wondered at that after two years and four months' continuous work amongst the people, without the interval of a Sunday, that I should have felt worn and fagged. In September last I went to visit my sister for a few days, and was taken ill, and thus prevented returning home on the Saturday as arranged. During my short absence I received the following letter from one of the members with no small satisfaction. He headed it with our medal motto, "All my springs are in Thee," Ps. lxxxvii. 7:—

"September 8th, 1860.

"DEAR MRS. W——,—I take the liberty to send a few words as a token of my sincere sympathy; and to inform you that you have an interest in our warmest prayers and desires—that you may be blessed with present grace, the grace that you need at this time, and that you may soon be restored to your active work of faith and labour of love.

"I was expecting to see you, ma'am, this evening at our prayer-meeting, but it is your Heavenly Father's will that it should be otherwise. I will try to go there to give my Amen for the prosperity of the object that you are so heartily engaged in; and though we shall feel the loss of your presence, and I am sure all will sincerely feel that, yet the Lord can and will bless you on the bed of pain, and bless us and make us a blessing to each other. May you, my very dear kind friend, and all of us as a Society, be brought to look more fixedly with the eye of faith on Christ, who is the Rock of Ages, the same yesterday, to-day, and for ever. And I am thankful that the source of your support and comfort is higher than earth. I often think with a degree of pleasure on that word, 'There is a river, the streams whereof shall make glad the city of God.' I saw dear Mr. Wightman. It was he that told me you were ill; I also saw my district-visitor,* who was struck to hear it, and we encouraged each other to go on in the strength of the Lord, as nothing would add so much to your comfort as to hear the cause was holding on and prospering, and every member doing his and her duty. We shall all be anxiously waiting to hear from you; and your welfare and comfort and restoration will be an object very near our hearts. May you enjoy much joy and peace in believing, and as your day so may your strength be.

"I am, my dear Mrs. W——,

"Yours gratefully,

——."

It was in June that I first felt the work was getting beyond my strength, or, rather, it was not so much my own work as the immense correspondence with personal strangers, which had so thoroughly taxed my strength, giving me no rest or leisure. Combining in myself the office of President, Committee, Treasurer, Secretary, Missionary, and Mother to the people, all the work devolved on me.

* One of the men in the Society.

My husband strongly advised a division of labour, but no one could be thought of to share it with me. At last, after much prayer, it seemed good to appoint a Scripture-reader from our ranks, and I fixed on H—— P——, in whom I knew full confidence could be placed. To my great comfort he acceded to my wish, and having given notice to his employer, he agreed to take the office on trial for three months, beginning his labours on August 1st, 1860. During those three months he was much encouraged by the kind welcome he received, and the good feeling that existed in the Society.

He found the majority in a hopeful state, ready and thankful for Bible-reading and prayer; some had come to Christ, and were giving evidence of growing in grace. The chief trial was that so little could be done amongst the men until after six o'clock in the evenings; he told me that he felt there was so much waste time on his hands, as far as working amongst the people was concerned, and that he felt he was taking the stipend to very little purpose. This greatly distressed him. "I find the women busy at their washing or baking, &c., the children at school, the husbands out. It is so much better to visit in the evenings from six till ten, when you can assemble the whole family. If eight or twelve Christian men from our ranks could be chosen out for missionary work, who would, for the love of Christ, give up two or three evenings a-week, much more work might be done, and it would be done *gratuitously*." He suggested that he would go back to his former employment, if I would allow him, adding, "I will gladly give three nights a-week myself to the missionary work."

I quite agree with H—— P——, that Scripture-readers will do little or no good unless they visit *at nights*. How can they otherwise ever know the *men* personally, or have a chance of winning *them* to Christ? It would be well if this matter were well considered, especially in large towns. Until the *men* are taken hold of, very little reformation can be effected in the households. It stands to reason that it must be so; and it is satisfactory to have the evidence of so competent a judge on the subject as the esteemed author of "Ragged Homes and How to Mend Them," who confessed to me that, until the husbands in the Kensington Potteries were influenced by her and the City Missionary ten months ago, the ragged homes continued as they were, for want of means to mend them, for nearly all the earnings of the husbands were previously spent in drink.

It was about this time that I received a letter from our friend, John ——, Scripture-reader at R——, from which the following extract is taken:—

. . . "Your prayers, I believe, are being felt and answered. Our little meetings increase every week, thanks be to God. We pray earnestly to God for a great blessing to rest on your Society, and also on yourself and family, my much-respected friend, Mrs. L—— and family, and her Society. It gives me great pleasure when the remembrance of her work is brought to my mind, and to look on the poor brands that have, by the grace of God, been snatched from the burning. Glory be to God! I believe that the same will be the case here. Please to continue to pray that the Holy Spirit may be poured out on this place. We commenced our Temperance Society on the 12th, and three men, two women, and two boys, signed the pledge. There have been no temperance lectures or tracts, or any excitement to cause it. We have three meetings a-week, a prayer-meeting at my own house on Tuesday nights, conducted by myself, one in the school-room, and one in an out part of the parish, conducted by our rector. The school-room meetings improve in attendance, as there are some who attend them that never went anywhere. I live in hopes that there will be a change in this place. We must sow the seed, and wait the Lord's appointed time, for we can do no good of ourselves without the aid of His Holy Spirit.

"My dear friend, I am very happy that you have help in your work, for you greatly need it. I think you have made a very good choice in Mr. P—— as Scripture-reader. We have remembered him at the throne of grace. I hope he will not only be made a blessing to his own household, but to all who hear him." . . .

The following is an extract from a letter received from a member of our Society residing in a large manufacturing town. He had been a total abstainer three years when he entered his name in our book. He was not in the habit of attending any place of worship then. I spoke to him as occasion offered, solemnly and earnestly; he always listened with great respect, but it was evident he had never felt his need of a Saviour. One night, after speaking to the people, I concluded with an earnest appeal to the undecided, saying, "Who will promise me that he will come *to-night* to Jesus for life and peace?" Amongst those who answered, "I will," was the writer of this letter. He, however, allowed the feeling to pass away. Next day I wrote from my sister's, where I had gone to spend a few days, to implore him not to delay coming to Christ. Through God's mercy, my letter eventually prevailed to decide him. He wrote me that a dark mist came over his sight as I spoke that night, the room became black, he felt the appeal was made for him specially, and he answered involuntarily a faint, "I will." He stifled the impression on his return home. But when my letter of September 10th reached him, it was too strong to resist. In his next letter he says, "I feel such happiness now,—thank God for it! We are now a praying family! I told my friends, the first month I abstained from drink, that I had felt more comfort that month than I had done the eighteen years I was a drunkard; but now, thank God! I tell them I've had more real solid happiness in Christ this three weeks, since I knew the Lord, than I ever had during the three years of my total abstinence. Dear lady, my whole trust and confidence is in God; and I can never forget the 10th of September, when I received your letter; I went in secret, as you told me, and prayed to my Father. I prostrated myself at the foot of Calvary, and asked Jesus fervently and anxiously to forgive me all my sins. I told him I was the vilest of sinners; I asked my Father, through His Son, to blot out all my sins and iniquities—to wash me in that precious blood, that I might be clean—to take my stony heart from me, and to give me a heart of flesh, that I might love Him, fear Him, and obey Him—to break the chains of sin that bound me so close to the world and Satan, that henceforth I might walk in the way of the righteous. Dear lady, I build upon God's promises. He says, 'Cast your burden upon Me, and I will bear it.' 'Whosoever believeth on Me hath everlasting life.'" [Here he enumerates many other promises.] "All these promises are beautiful and encouraging to a poor sinner like me. I rise and lie down praising His holy name. He is my Father, my Instructor, my Guide, my Deliverer.

God, in His love to me, has sent the Holy Spirit the Comforter to console my anguishing soul. All seems to me as you told me, dear lady,—all is comfort and joy and rest where Christ is. Where He is not there is no rest. I thank God for all things through Christ. Bless His holy Name! The devil goes about like a roaring lion, seeking whom he may devour; he has battled hard with the Spirit of God within me; my besetting sins seem more before me, but I thank God He gives me the victory over them. When I think how our Lord was tempted, and how He said, 'Get thee behind me, Satan, for *it is written*,' &c., and again, how Joseph said, 'How can I do this great wickedness and sin against God?' is it not encouraging for a poor mortal like me? And then I ask my Father to send His Holy Spirit to strengthen me, His dust.

"Dear lady, now God has been so good to me as to change my wicked and sinful heart, the least I can do for my Father is to get others to come to Him for succour and life." [Here he mentioned two families whom he had been instrumental in bringing to Christ. One had been an enemy of his, and they had desired him to tell me that they had now learned to pray, and were full of joy and peace in believing.] "Dear lady, I want others now to know God and to reject the world. Believe me, as you were the instrument in God's hands of my coming to Jesus, I wish to show you what the Spirit is doing by me. Excuse the imperfections of a reclaimed drunkard and a reclaimed sinner. God be with you and bless you. . . ."

Some weeks after receiving this letter, I heard from John Waldron's pastor, telling me that he is working like a missionary right and left, speaking for Jesus, and that his wife is become a partaker of the same grace with him. To God be all the praise.

"I wish you would have meetings for inquirers, something like the class-meetings in our communion," said the foreman of a timber-yard, who is a Nonconformist, and who, though not a member of our Society, feels a lively interest in our progress. Some of the most noisy and drunken men working with him have joined our ranks, and, by the grace of God, have become changed men.

"It's wonderful the quiet in our yard now! those men used to be fighting, cursing, and swearing; now you only hear words about what they've heard in church or the meetings—a bit of a hymn or a text of Scripture, which they talk over."

"Just come and see how our minister conducts his class-meeting in our chapel," said James Fuller, a member of our Society, some months after, to me; "I can't tell why you won't try to have one yourself."

It seemed narrow-minded not to take a lesson from a man because he differs from us.

"No one will speak to you, nor take any notice of you—you have only to sit quiet and listen."

I accompanied James Fuller—and I must acknowledge that my prejudice vanished. The deep humility of all present, and the wise and apt quotations from Scripture, suited to each individual case, struck me as most remarkable. In wise hands such a meeting must have a rich blessing. I am sure no *hypocrite* could attend a second time so close a scrutiny; it would be uncongenial to any except the sincere and earnest seeker after Jesus.

I adopted the plan, forming separate classes for men and women, limiting each to twelve persons. My husband takes one of the former fortnightly for me; he comes from this class with a radiant face, and tells me it is the sweetest hour he spends: every one speaks freely of his trials, struggles, &c., asks counsel on special occasions, and gets encouragement from the treasury of God's word. The same truths which appear of *general* application when heard from the pulpit, go home straight to the heart when spoken at these meetings. If such were generally adopted, I believe many an earnest and loving heart might be kept in our communion who, for want of the help and comfort such meetings afford, join Nonconformist congregations.

Two Wesleyans have joined in communion with our church since we began these meetings.

Our Society.

"Jesus, Lord, we look to Thee,
Let us in Thy Name agree;
Make us of one heart and mind,—
Courteous, pitiful, and kind.
Let us for each other care,
Each the other's burden bear
Free from anger and from pride,
Let us each in God abide."

CHAPTER XIV.

It was with no small surprise I heard lately from a gentleman in London, that a friend of his had spent a few hours in Shrewsbury on purpose to glean some information about our Society, that he had gone to several shops and had asked questions, but found that no information could be obtained. Nobody knew whether there was an Association bearing the name of St. Alkmond's Total Abstinence Society! I could not help thinking of a lady whom I once asked to accompany me to a Missionary Meeting, and who declined, saying, "I do not think the Missionary Society is doing any good; Major —— dined with us last week; you know he has been in India nearly thirty years, and he assured me he had never seen a missionary in his life, and he does not believe there are any." I answered, "Have you ever read any published accounts of the Bishop of Calcutta's Visitations?" and I sent her some printed extracts of an address given by Lieut.-Col. Herbert Edwardes, K.C.B., in which he speaks of missionary work in India.

We now number upwards of four hundred and fifty men, more than two hundred women, and four hundred juveniles.

People ask me, "Are any public-houses shut up?" I answer, "*Does not the King live for ever?*" We who reside in Shrewsbury may notice public-houses shut up, because the landlords are "sold up," but new names appear after a few days, and the houses look as they did before.* It must be remembered that the members of our Society are a scattered people; perhaps two may live in a street, where forty other families may be drinking; they extend over a large area, the town of Shrewsbury and its suburbs.

A clergyman, who is a personal stranger, wrote to me after purposely visiting Shrewsbury to see our work. He did not call at the Vicarage; he visited Butcher Row as a matter of course, and seeing that locality very repulsive in its exterior, he was sure it could not be the street named in the little record of our labours. Why not? Who expects any whole street to be christianised? God is *taking out* from the mass a people for His glory in this dispensation of election. Here one, there another, is brought out, and the rest continue as they were. Is it not so in *families?* How seldom a whole family is brought to Jesus! Why should His work amongst us be different from what it is elsewhere, and has been in all past ages?

Again, the total abstainers do not continue to reside

* At present the "Wheat Sheaf" and "Circus Tavern" are closed!

in dirty, disagreeable localities. Butcher Row will therefore continue to look the same as it does, whilst its five public, or beer-houses, and its slaughter-houses continue, unless the owners of the cottages give the people a chance of bettering their condition by re-building the street, with some regard to cleanliness, decency, and ventilation. Is it not a shame to see slaughter-houses, &c., allowed in the middle of a town, in close proximity to the dwellings of the poor?

St. Alkmond's Total Abstinence Society is, nevertheless, a FACT.

It is a sight to comfort one's heart to see twenty male communicants and fifty other regular attendants added to our congregation, besides those who are attending other churches or chapels in Shrewsbury. Some of these had not been in a place of worship for fifteen, twenty, or thirty years, except on some rare occasion.

We have twelve district-visitors, from amongst our members, some of whom take their tracts *weekly* to their people, encouraging them by kind words and friendly counsel. And this is no small labour, when it is remembered that to visit forty families, one must go over much ground as the families are scattered one here, one there, not like an ordinary district where every house is visited in succession. These men work gratuitously.

Then there are those who distribute tracts in

streets where no members reside, and where very few, if any, attend a place of worship. A stonemason has undertaken to work in Butcher's Row. These men have opportunities of speaking for Jesus, and of reading the Scriptures with prayer. Sometimes they meet old associates, the surprise occasioned by such encounters is graphically described by my friend John Ithell, the tailor: "I had such a happy time in my district last Sunday, there were several men at home whom I had never chanced to find in before; they had once been drinking companions of mine, and they did stare above a bit on seeing me! They had no idea who brought them the tracts, as their wives did not know me. They said, to think of *me* turning tract-distributor! they never heard such a thing! So we had a good talk, and I am in hopes of their turning to be different, and there were two others whom I visit who have signed since last Sunday; that did please me a good deal, I can tell you!"

It was mentioned in the last chapter that H—— P——, our Scripture-reader, was discouraged by the small amount of work he was able to accomplish amongst the *men* before six o'clock P.M., and that he proposed we should choose some others from our ranks, to share with him the missionary work at nights, who should give their time gratuitously. At the close of his three months' trial he felt his conviction strengthened; so I acceded to his wish, and he returned to his old employment, and I met some of the men on whose judgment and Christian principles I could fully depend, and upon naming the project to them, they willingly acquiesced, glad to have an opportunity of working for Christ amongst their brothers. H—— P—— was present, and agreed to give up three nights a-week gratuitously. Some could only spare one, others two evenings a-week—most of them could give two hours on Sunday afternoons. We divided the work into equal portions, and put down more names, for we found that we should need a larger staff of labourers than we had imagined.

We agreed to meet weekly for conference and counsel, and that each man should bring me a written journal of his work. But here a difficulty arose: which evening could be spared for meeting together? I could not give up Monday or Friday nights, as I visit the members at their homes then. On Thursday night we have our women's working party, and on Tuesday our "Reading;" every Wednesday evening there is our lecture in church, and after that, at half-past eight o'clock, my communicants' meeting, for men and women in alternate weeks. On Saturday we have the Men's Sick Fund, and prayer-meeting afterwards. At last, after much consideration, we fixed on Tuesday night *after* the "Reading," as the men wished always to be present on that occasion.

This agency is too recently established to speak

of results, but the men who have undertaken the work have, we believe, given themselves to Christ. We confidently look for and expect a rich blessing on their labours. Some of them were drunkards, others never were. I give one sample of their journals, by which it will be seen that not only are the members visited, but the home-heathen around them are also searched out, and gathered together for hearing the word of God and prayer.

"*Sunday, Sept. 30th.*—After praying that God would bless our labours, I started to take a tract to each member's house, by way of introducing myself, and explaining my intended visits for the future. I was greatly encouraged in finding that all parties were highly pleased at the arrangements. The last house I called at was —— ——, where I invited several of his neighbours in, and a most interesting meeting took place. The parties present were, a sweep, a coalheaver, a nailor, and Mr. —— ——. I knew the coalheaver to be a notorious swearer, the others knew nothing about the immortality of the soul. They had all been to church two or three times in their lives, but candidly confessed that they knew nothing whatever about what the minister had been preaching. It was quite a mystery to them. I prayed that God would direct me how to proceed with such as these poor heathen were; and I believe He heard me, for I found no lack of words, and by their anxious inquiries since (for I have had several meetings since), I find that what I said was not forgotten.

"*Monday, Oct.* 1*st.*—I went to the —— and read the tract called 'The Two Willies,' a story of Lucknow. While reading it, an old man, very much intoxicated, burst into the kitchen, swearing vehemently. He didn't expect to meet with such a party, for he appeared paralysed. I invited him to sit on my chair by my si le, as there was no other seat for him, and he said, 'Well, I don't mind if I do.' I took no further notice of him, but continued reading; and when I read about the swearer in the hospital, how hardened he was, and the happy death of his son, he groaned aloud, and at last got up, and looked me hard in the face (I thought he was going to strike me), he said, 'I conna stand it any longer, it's too much of a thing,' and rushed out of the place as abruptly as he came in. He has since asked after me, and I intend to look him up; the other three were greatly affected by the story read. I then read the story of blind Bartimeus, and compared his blindness with the natural blindness of man.

"After offering up prayer I came away.

"*Thursday, Oct.* 4*th.*—I had a beautiful evening with Mr. —— and his family; and J. —— and his family."

Four times a-year we have a social meeting. In January our anniversary takes place in the form of a tea-party in the Music Hall, when clergymen and other friends give addresses.

Last Show Monday we went to Llangollen. Many vivid pictures remain in our memory. We shall never forget the happy groups on the top of Castel Dinas Bran, where dear old George Raymond said, "It's worth a twelvemonth's close work to have such a day as this! It's something to think of for months after!" There we all dined, each family having turned sutler. There we received as a memorial of our trip the signatures of some friends who had joined the excursion. I fear we forgot to look at the magnificent expanse of scenery, the glimpse into the heavenly Canaan, given in foretaste as we looked at the many dear and happy faces around us, overswept and eclipsed all earthly glories. Then there was the quiet walk to Vale Crucis Abbey, reminding some of us of the walk to Emmaus, as we talked of Jesus by the way; and the lovely sail of six miles in large open boats holding one hundred each, to and from the station, through the far-famed Vale of Llangollen; and the exquisite beauty of scenery which tempted some of us to get out and walk when we were on the aqueduct, and those sweet hymns sung by the way, attracting crowds to the banks of the canal, especially the men working at the iron-works, who thronged to catch a glimpse of us as our boats passed quickly by. And our friends from Chirk and Halford were with us, bringing the members of their societies, scions of our own. Which of us will forget the hymns sung under the tent after tea, or the Hallelujah chorus after sunset when the dark clouds burst into a sudden storm as we stood at the Llangollen Road Station waiting for our train, or " God save the Queen " on arriving at Shrewsbury, all spirits being exuberant, although every one admitted we had each walked about nine miles, and the hearty farewells and graspings of hands, as each family turned homewards, such a contrast to common excursion trips when so many return home drunk or quarrelsome.

At our last tea-party, Sept. 25th, the Dean of Carlisle cheered us with his presence and hearty sympathy, much to the delight of all the members, who will long remember with gratitude the kind sentiments he expressed towards them.

We were glad on that occasion to exhibit the beautiful banners presented to us by the members of a Total Abstinence Society in Birmingham,* who came two hundred strong to spend a day with us last summer.

A word about our choir. It is self-organized, and composed of members, they sing extremely well. One

* From Legge Street.

of our most favourite pieces is the beautiful hymn "Haste to the Rescue," adapted from "The Macedonian Cry," by our friend Mrs. L——, which has been set to music by William Griffiths, a member of our choir. It is arranged for four voices, with a very sweet harmony. We can strongly recommend its adoption by all Temperance Societies. It has also been translated into Welsh by a friend at Llangollen. It may be obtained from us, or through the publisher.*

Our ranks are composed of working men of every grade. There are smiths, strikers, nailors, tin-plate-workers, lead-millers, iron-moulders, tailors, shoemakers, railway officials, and some employed in making the locomotives for the same; also engine-drivers, firemen, stonemasons, sawyers of wood and stone, bricklayers, labourers, butchers, hairdressers, tanners, dyers, carpenters, joiners, turners, fishmongers, office clerks, navvies, &c., millwrights, painters, waiters, gentlemen's servants, grooms, &c. We have also a resident surgeon in our ranks, and two local clergymen, one of whom is the chaplain of the county gaol; and a military officer; and several ladies who do not live in this county.

It would be well to mention that one of our chief hindrances has nearly ceased; *it is very rarely that a medical man now ventures to recommend stimulants to any one in our ranks!* Indeed, we have all had such

* Mr. W. Tweedie, No. 337 Strand.

good health, through the mercy of God, that we have hardly needed a doctor. And so thorough is our conviction that stimulants are unnecessary and hurtful rather than beneficial, that I do not think we should have much faith in any one who prescribed them!

Another fact must not be omitted. The notion that nursing mothers require stimulants is becoming exploded in our ranks. Many a good wife and mother has shown me her baby with great delight, "Don't you think, ma'am, our *teetotal baby* is the best of the lot?" Certainly they have thriven wondrously, being superior in health, strength, and good looks, to other children of the same age.

We gave the women who attended the working party a tea-drinking last Whit Monday, when we broke up for the season. We have just resumed these meetings, and, as those who joined us were some of the best wives and needle-women in the Society, we have enlisted their services to help us in instructing the factory girls in needle-work. Miss H——, who kindly took all the business part off my hands, will still give her valuable services, and some other friends have volunteered their aid.

We ask every one who reads this chapter to lift up an earnest prayer that the motto which heads it may be fulfilled to each member of our Society.

"How do you distinguish the members belonging to your Society at your pleasure-trips and festive meetings?" asked a friend one day.

"I know them all personally; but strangers may easily recognise us by the badge we wear, sometimes it is a nosegay, sometimes a ribbon."

"Would not a medal be better?"

This was a delightful thought, and quite new to us all. So we resolved to have a medal of our own.

The accompanying letter to my sister gives a history of it, and of a most unexpected but gratifying event which arose out of our plan.

"St. Alkmond's Vicarage, August 4, 1860.

"MY DEAREST CAROLINE,—I told you that I was having a medal struck for our Society. What do you think? The grateful people, as soon as they heard of it, had a select meeting, 'unknowings to the missus,' at which they unanimously agreed to get the first impression taken in pure gold, and formed into an elegant brooch for me. The presentation took place yesterday. But before I tell you anything about that, you must look at the accompanying sketch.* The rock represents our Saviour. Is not the motto beautiful? Do you notice the goblet cast down at the woman's feet, with an adder around it? On the obverse you may see our form of pledge on

* See title page, where a wood cut of the medal, on a small scale, is given.

the scroll; a hand from earth is receiving it. The dove, with the rays of glory, denotes the necessity of the Holy Spirit's help to keep us from any sin. The Bible, crown, and sceptre below, with the ship on the sea, are emblematic of England—her religion, constitution, and commerce; thus hopefully looking forward to the *national* adoption of our total-abstinence principles. 'The Lord bless thee, and grant thee grace to keep thy promise,' is inscribed around, with the name and date of our Society below.

"I took our motto, 'All my springs are in Thee,' for my subject last Sunday night. It is wonderful how the dear people, whose hearts were brim-full of the coming presentation, could listen so attentively without letting out the slightest hint of their secret.

"There being only six words in our motto, each word formed a separate head. I give you a sketch of what was said.

"'*All my springs are in* THEE.' (Taking the last word to begin with.) *Thee, i.e.* Christ. Why?—Because, 'It pleased the Father that in Him should all fulness dwell.' 'In Him are hid all the treasures of wisdom and knowledge.'

"If 'All my springs are in Thee,' what is the condition of all those who are independent of Christ? who have no desire towards Him, no love? Awful, beyond conception. Thirsty, empty, unsatisfied, poor, wretched, miserable, and that, not only now, but for ever.

"'*All my springs are* IN . . .' Not only from, nor by, though this is included, but more than this,—IN Christ. Let us beware of seeking it in *self*, or in the *creature.* '*He* is made of God unto us Wisdom, Righteousness, Sanctification, and Redemption.' We must *come to Him*,—nay, more, we must *abide in Him.*

"'*All my springs* ARE . . .' Not *shall be*, though that is also true, but *present* enjoyment and experience. *Now* in our wilderness state, in 'a land of drought.' *Now* in our time of need. If so precious *now*, what shall it be *hereafter* when we shall see Him face to face?

"'*All my* SPRINGS . . .' Jesus is the source of life, joy, and peace; of strength, comfort, and hope; of grace, and power, &c. &c. A fountain that shall never fail; ever fresh, ever satisfying. Eternity cannot fathom its depth; he that drinketh of this water shall never thirst, for the Holy Ghost the Comforter 'shall be in him a well of water springing up into eternal life.'

"'*All* MY . . .' A matter of personal experience, not *our* springs, nor *their* springs, but MY springs.

"'ALL . . .' Not some, nor yet *sometimes*, but *always*, and *all*, in joy, in sorrow, in trial, in temptation. We eschew from henceforth *all* 'broken cisterns,' —and deliberately and for ever resolve that, 'out of His fulness,' alone we will receive, 'and grace for grace.'

"Well, to return to the presentation. One of the

"O! look at the Garden."

Annals Rescued. p. 225

women suggested to Charles Wilding the evening before, 'You must tell the missus in time, or she'll be off a mile and a half from home at eight o'clock, Friday being one of her visiting nights amongst the members.' It was then agreed that my husband should tell me in due time to prevent such a catastrophe. So I thought it would be nice to have some thorough-hearted friends to witness the sight; it would be so much more pleasant than to have it all to one's self. We therefore asked Sir George and Lady —— and their family, and Mrs. L——, to spend the evening with us. We sat talking quietly after tea (of course I was longing to know the mysterious arrangements beforehand), when, suddenly, just before eight o'clock, one of our party, chancing to look out of the window, exclaimed, 'Oh, look at the garden!' It was a sight, indeed! Two hundred people had ranged themselves round the gravel-walk, forming a circle. Two of the men were placing forms for the ladies. We put on our bonnets quickly, and I lingered for a few moments to ask God's blessing on the honest, warm-hearted friends met together to do me honour. A messenger came to hasten me, 'Please, ma'am, they are all waiting for you.'

"It was impossible to look unmoved at their kindly faces as I hurried into the centre of the group. Our total abstinence choir struck up a piece they had prepared. Sir George —— then presented the medal.

You know he is one of our pledged members, so it was quite in order. When I looked into the casket and saw the medal, it was a great relief to hear the choir begin another piece of music.

"It is wonderful what refinement and delicacy of feeling these grateful people have. One of them had said to my husband, 'We know she'll be greatly overcome when she sees it, so we must give her time to recover by singing another piece.' But I could not 'recover' quite so speedily. Too many thoughts crowded upon me. The costliness of the offering (they had subscribed, I afterwards heard, upwards of twenty guineas) took me by surprise. Here were we standing on the site of our early garden meetings, when our numbers were but small. Before me stood the same dear old faces, both men and women, faithful and firm as ever, and 'one is not;' the thought of Richard Stedman, and many a talk with him in this very spot of that Saviour in whose blessed presence we believe he now is; and then, the progress and consolidation of our work, the many before me whom I knew to be fellow-heirs of eternal life. Could any one expect me to be unmoved? I began, 'All of you come close round me;' at that moment my husband joined us, he had come away from the clerical meeting on purpose to be present. He came and gave me his arm. The people closed round us, the women to my left in a group, not one without tears in her eyes.

Seeing that I could not get on, a hundred kindly voices from amongst the men gently said, 'Cheer up, cheer up!' all looking so full of love and interest. I did at last thank them heartily, and told them where my thoughts had been wandering, which affected the old members to tears, and ended by an earnest prayer, that none then standing before us might be wanting in the day of Christ's glory, to which all present added a fervent 'Amen.' Forgetting that the arrangements were in other hands, I said, 'Do let us sing our favourite hymn,

"'There is a Fountain filled with blood,'

and we had the chorus which we love so much,—

"'I do believe, I will believe,
That Jesus died for me,
And on the cross He shed His blood,
That I might happy be;'

in which all joined with thrilling earnestness. Those who have never heard them sing cannot form any idea of it. I never heard such singing in any church as we have at our meetings.

"Dear Charles then closed with prayer, and every one (the men still bareheaded) knelt. It was a sight indeed to remember. The clock struck nine. The sun had long set, and we could hardly distinguish one another's countenances.

"The choir then sang, 'God save the Queen,' and every one grasped my hand as if we were never to meet again, and gave me a hearty blessing. Several of the people saying, 'You'll wear that medal every day, we hope.' 'Yes, I will wear it every day.' Was not this a foretaste of eternal glory? Shall we not all meet around His Throne? God grant that we may of His infinite mercy, for Jesus Christ's sake . . . .

"Your loving sister,

"JULIA B. W.

"P.S.—To-day they carried off my brooch, to add the inscription, 'With the love of the members to their President, Mrs. Wightman, Aug. 3, 1860.' Sure no medal presented by royal hands was ever half so precious!"

In the following week I presented a white metal medal to each member in the Society, who was six months old and upwards, making a distinction between those given to the men and to the women by adding a different ribbon, the "Indian mutiny" ribbon being selected for the men, the "Syrian" for the women.

Amongst the letters received in acknowledgment of their medals from members who have left Shrewsbury, I add the following:—

"———, Sussex.

"MADAM,—I hope you will not think me bold in taking the liberty of writing to you, but when I received my medal I thought it my duty to write and thank you for it, and also for the kindness and favours which you do bestow from time to time upon the Society which you have established in Shrewsbury. I hope the good work is still progressing amongst you there, and that you are winning many souls from that end to which the intoxicating cup leads daily.

"I must say, that I am very much delighted with the medal and the reading upon it; and as it is your prayer that the Lord would give us grace to keep our promise, I feel that I can tell you that He gives me large supplies of that grace.

"Since I left Shrewsbury in March last, I have been where the intoxicating cup has free course; and during the past summer, whilst business has called me from home, and I have been stopping one or two nights together in some of the large towns in Sussex and the adjoining county, I have taken up my abode in some of the inns most convenient for those that were with me, and the cup has been freely and liberally put to me, but I could with firmness reply, 'No, thank you, I would rather not;' and the voice would be heard, 'Drink, young fellow,' or, 'What will you have to drink?'

"It often appears to me a great mystery how ever I can so firmly resist it, but I forgot that the Lord is true to His promise, 'My grace is sufficient for thee.' Madam, I do not think that I shall ever repent joining your Society, for I firmly believe that it is not known to man the wickedness that is committed by intoxicating drinks: I have cause to believe that it is *one* of the greatest curses upon our land, if not *the* greatest. And now, as I am many miles from you, I cannot do anything in assisting you in that way, which the Apostle Paul speaks of in one of his Epistles, 'knowing therefore the terror of the Lord, we persnade men,' but I feel that I can pray for you all, and I do pray that the Lord may bless you abundantly, and give you strength to go on from conquering to conquer,—I hope my dear little brother is still firm, and will keep so to his life's end. And may we all at last be safely landed on Canaan's shore.

"Please to excuse and forgive all imperfections.

"Believe me to remain, yours, ...

"———."

From Mr. and Mrs. ———, who were parishioners of ours, and left Shrewsbury in 1859.

"August 20th, 1860.

"Honoured Lady,—We beg to acknowledge the receipt of two beautiful medals on the 16th, for which we thank you very much indeed. We often talk about the very nice meetings that you have; we miss them very much. We should like to meet once again, if the Lord permits. We are very glad to hear of your being so prosperous; may it long continue, and we are sure the Lord has blessed the cause.

We have great cause for thankfulness on our part, and we do praise God for all. He is so gracious to us. We are glad to hear that —— is doing so well. I hope his wife and family are well, I feel assured they must feel the comfort and the benefit of his keeping the pledge. Please to give our united love to all old members, they are too numerous to mention; I am sure they must all have been delighted to hear your account of Mr. Gough's last lecture in London; it must have been a very interesting sight, and a very pleasing one, to see him presented with so beautiful a Bible;—he will have his reward, and may God bless him, and all that devote themselves to such a good cause.

"I must thank you very kindly for your letter, and the great comfort it gave us to read it over and over again; it was as a cordial to a drooping spirit in a strange land. Oh, that we should ever doubt our ever-present Saviour! But our own hearts are prone to wander. We think your selection of ribbon for the medals very good. I really cannot think how ever you do continue, but it is the Lord that worketh with you, and long may you be spared to work, and see the seed spring and grow up to maturity in the members of your Society to the glory of God. We shall store our medals, and never may we have cause to look back with shame and confusion, but store in our hearts the good we have received; and may God bless you, and dear Mr. Wightman, and bless him in all his sermons, and may St. Alkmond's church be a marked church; and as it has been blessed with Christian men for past years, so may it continue, is the prayer of your humble servants.

"We join in united love to all, and

"Believe us ever your faithful servants,

"T. and M. ———."

I was calling one day upon John Reading, to thank him for his share in the present given to me, "Oh, ma'am," said he, "you should have seen Humphrey Jackson; he was so resolved not to be out of that job, that he schemed how he could any road manage to give towards it. You see, he's not well off. So he thought to himself, 'What can I give up so as to save a bit of money towards her medal?' and he said, 'There's the *smoking*, that runs away with a good bit of money! So he resolved that he would deny his-self of that, for the pleasure of subscribing to your medal. And he found that he could do without the tobacco altogether. So he paid his money in; and would you believe it, soon after he found himself twelve shillings and sixpence in pocket! And he does without smoking now altogether!"

Here is an example of the old adage, "Where there's a will there's a way!" And what a lesson is here taught us all, on the subject of self-denial, as a help to *Christian charity*. How many of us content ourselves with only giving to God of that which costs us nothing! May the Lord deepen our faith and love, and enable us to give *ourselves* to Him, and then nothing will be too great a sacrifice to spend for His honour and glory.

On the subject of smoking, I add just a few words.

It is an acknowledged fact, on the highest medical authority, that among the causes of mental disease, one of the greatest is the excessive use of tobacco. Loss of memory takes place, in an extraordinary degree, in the smoker, even more so than in the drunkard.

It is harder to abstain from the use of tobacco, when once acquired, than from the use of intoxicating drinks. Nevertheless, some men in our Society have vanquished this habit, and others are doing so by degrees.

Prevention is better than cure. Our juveniles take this form of pledge, "I promise, by the help of God, to abstain from all intoxicating drink, and from the use of tobacco in any form."

The Women's Testimony.

"A good report making the bones fat."

CHAPTER XV.

It may be supposed, from the prominence given in these pages to the men, that our interest and sympathy are exclusively enlisted on their behalf. This is not the case. And two facts should be borne in mind.

First, the *men* have been hitherto almost wholly neglected, because few clergymen, district-visitors, or Scripture-readers, visit the working-classes at the hours when the husbands are at home.

Secondly, failing to get hold of the men, the ragged and miserable homes continue as they were; for until the husbands' wages are rescued from the public-house, the most thrifty and careful wife has not wherewithal to supply home necessaries or comforts.

Mrs. Grafton was taken ill suddenly on Tuesday night. I did not hear of it till Thursday. Next day found me by her bedside. The thorough comfort and cleanliness of her little room struck me. She was sitting up in bed sewing. "I'm a deal better to-day, thank you," she said, smiling, as I asked all the particulars. After praying with her, the tears stood in her eyes as she spoke with the most fervent gratitude of the change wrought in her home.

"We've been married seventeen years, and nobody knows but God and my own heart all I have gone through with his drunkenness." I remembered having heard of his having turned her and the little children into the street many a night, and that she had sometimes taken shelter at a relation's for a week together, dreading the drunken rage of him who had vowed to love, honour, and cherish her.

"But you must not dwell upon the past, dear friend. Your husband has stood firm for more than a year, and I believe the grace of God has touched his heart now, and that he will never go back to sin."

"Oh! I'm sure of that. He is so kind and good to me now, and he prays with me now every day. It cost him a good bit to begin to pray before the children. He had attended your meeting three months at least before he got courage to kneel down in their presence. He used to say his prayers after he got into bed, that they might not notice him. But one morning my eldest little girl came down-stairs as I was getting breakfast ready, and she said, 'Oh, mother, there's father kneeling by the bedside, saying his prayers, just as we children do in school on Sundays!'"

It struck me forcibly, if little children never see their parents pray, will not the lesson learned in the

Sunday-school be cast aside as soon as they grow up, as one of the childish things to be given up when they become men and women!

Letters received during a fortnight in Edinburgh, the wives having heard that some people said I ignored *them*. Many others, equally kind, were received. They were sent for publication. I make no apology for the fond partiality of these grateful and affectionate people, whose hearty expressions towards me I could not hurt their feelings by omitting.

"Shrewsbury, Nov. 1st, 1860.

"Ever dear Lady,—I have to bless God that I ever heard your name, for you have been the cause of making my home a happy one. My husband has been a member now going on for three years, and, bless God, the last two years I have had more happiness than ever I had in all my life. I have been a wife seventeen years last February, and never knew what comfort was till my husband was one of your members. I myself signed the pledge, not because I was a drunkard, but to encourage my husband to hold fast that blessed hope of heaven which he now possesses, thank God. The first step to the change in him was through giving up the drink and signing the pledge, and having such a kind lady as you to visit amongst us; and may God grant you many years amongst us!

I wish I had more time to write. I could fill a book myself. I must conclude with our hearty love to you, dear lady, and may God send you safe back to us again! "SARAH REYNOLDS AND FAMILY,"

Wife of a bricklayer.

From a tanner's wife:—

"October 31, 1860.

"DEAREST LADY,—I hope these few poor simple lines will find you in good health, and taking a little comfortable rest after your long and laborious work, day after day and night after night, with us poor people.

"Dearest lady, we shall all feel your absence very keenly, and miss your kind presence and sympathy. I don't know whatever we should do without you; we should have no one to come in and cheer us, and encourage us in our afflictions; no one to console and comfort us in our sorrow. I shall never find words to express my heartfelt gratitude to you for all the comfort you have brought into my home. I think of the time you visited me when my dear baby was ill; and when the blessed Lord thought fit to call her to Himself, how you sympathized in our sorrow, and how you came through the frost and the snow last year to visit me in my confinement! I pray the great God to reward you for all your goodness.

"My husband and children all join with me in kind love to you, and in wishing you all the happiness this world can afford; we all unite in praying that you may have a safe return, for we are quite lost without you.

"I remain,
"Your humble servant,
"MARY JONES."

From John Pope:—

"DEAR MADAM,—Perhaps you may be disappointed in not receiving this letter from my wife, but she is so busy going round to the parties mentioned in your letter this morning. Every one of the wives would like to write a volume, if they were able to do so, to express their gratitude to you for the benefit they have received through your kindness and love to them, and through their husbands joining your Society. My wife cried when she came in from visiting them, whilst telling me how they shed tears, and spoke of you to her. . . .

"Oh! if any one doubts in the smallest degree that the wife has not been even more cared for than the husband, we will pay their expenses to come and judge for themselves, by visiting them personally, for words cannot do justice in the slightest degree to the grateful outpouring of hearts full of thankfulness towards one who has *hasted and rescued* them from misery here, and God grant it may be from eternal misery hereafter!

"Mr. Powell wishes me to mention that when engaged by you as Scripture-reader, very often the wives spoke of your kindness with tears in their eyes. He joins my wife and myself in dutiful obedience and remembrance.

"Believe me,

"Dear madam, yours obediently,

"JOHN POPE."

From Mrs. Pope:—

". . . Mrs. R. Richards says she regrets she has never had an opportunity of expressing her heartfelt gratitude and thanks for the great good she has derived from joining your Society, as it was at your meetings she found Jesus; and she begs me tell you that her home, though poor, is *very rich*, and her prayers ascend night and morning to heaven, that God might abundantly bless you for your work and labour of love."

From the same:—

"I called on Mrs. George Raymond to-day. I am sorry to say I found her very unwell, but she begged me to say that she never could find words to express her gratitude for the change you had been the means of effecting in her home; she says she shall have cause to bless you throughout eternity.

"I saw also Mrs. Wall; she said there is a blessed change in her home, not only temporally, but especially in spiritual things, since she and her husband joined your Society. They both earnestly pray you may long be spared to carry on so noble a work."

From Mrs. James, the wife of a tailor: —

"October 31, 1860.

"DEAR MADAM,—I know very well that there are plenty of people who do not know the good that has been done in Shrewsbury since the commencement of our Society, but were they to have known many of our members, both men, and women, and children, before they became members, and to know them now, they would not think them the same people. Your work amongst the men was a great thing, but amongst the women, in my opinion, still greater. Your visiting their houses so often, they try to keep their homes as tidy as possible, which before they had no heart to do anything. I feel very sorry for some of our new members, for when they look at the comfortable homes of our old members, they are almost afraid they will never be like them; but I encourage them as much as I can. It's heart-rending to look at their poor children, but I hope our juveniles will exceed our adults in number. I think it is a great deal in conversing with our neighbours, that has caused my two friends who live close by to have joined us. The two women were telling me how kind you had spoken to their husbands, and how kind you had been to visit them. You do not know how much good you are doing; in fact, there is nothing you can do better than to encourage the women, for it makes the men better members.

"I must now conclude, hoping the Almighty will watch over you and guard you in the hour of danger, and bring you safe home to us all.

"I remain,

"Yours faithfully,

"ELLEN JAMES."

From Mrs. Thomason, the wife of a labourer:—

"November 1, 1860.

"DEAR PRESIDENT,—This is to certify that it is to you, under God, that I owe all my present comforts, and these are not a few in comparison of what I had two years ago, when first I became acquainted with you.

"I, for one, have cause to bless the hour that the Lord put it in your heart to do for such poor mortals as I am. No one in the world would have done more than you have done. There are scores of my fellow-sisters can testify the same, for which I sincerely hope the Lord will reward you for all your labour for the good of us poor fallen creatures.

"I trust that this will find you in good health and enjoying yourself, and that you will be brought home safe again. We seem as if lost when you are away; you seem as if you were the life of us all.

"Dear President, I am happy to say I am quite well, and feel happy to have to subscribe myself,

"Your humble and ever indebted servant,

"SARAH THOMASON."

From Mrs. Ithell, a tailor's wife:—

"November 2, 1860.

"DEAR MADAM,—As you expressed a wish to hear from any of your members, I am very glad of this opportunity of writing to you, hoping that this will find Mr. Wightman and yourself quite well. I have been married eighteen years, and during that time have suffered every sorrow that drink could bring, loss of goods and loss of health.

"But since my husband joined your then small, but now noble, Society, we have had nothing but peace and happiness. When I see him now every night and morning kneeling down to pray by my bedside, I cannot but compare the difference between my last confinement and this. Then he had been drinking a fortnight, and I almost lost my life. I know you will be glad to hear that I was confined on Wednesday morning, and am going on well. I cannot but lift up my heart to God in thankfulness, and pray that your life may be spared many years, for the sake of the poor drunkards and their families.

"As I am very weak, I know you will excuse my writing a short letter. My husband and I join in sending our duty to Mr. Wightman and yourself.

"I remain,

"Your grateful and humble servant,

"MARY ITHELL."

From Mrs. Gaunt, wife of a factory operative, and foreman: —

"My Dear President,—I am thankful to God that ever I had a knowledge of you; for, through being induced to join the pledge, I have been rescued from destruction; and I believe I should soon have been in hell. Sorrow had driven me to that cursed drink, from which I felt no power to refrain. But, through your instrumentality in the hands of God, I can say I am now what I am, and that is very different to what I was two years ago, for I was then a miserable woman; but now, thanks be to God and your never-failing kindness, I have every needful blessing.

"I trust you are well and enjoying yourself, and that the Lord will bring you safe back again to the field of your labours, for there is a great work for you to do. May the Lord give you health and strength to perform it! My dear President, I am thankful to have to style myself,

"Your humble and indebted servant,

"Marion Gaunt.

"P.S.—I wish to state that I was the first to join in my family, and through that, my husband and son have done the same, thank God. And I trust, through His strength, we shall ever remain firm."

I will close this chapter with an extract from a letter just received from the Rev. H. C——, with further tidings about his Scripture-reader, John —— and his wife:—

"November –, 1860.

"... We are going on steadily, and I think surely. Our own band who have signed the pledge keep most steadfast, and, moreover, are, I trust, growing in grace and knowledge. They are diligent in the means of grace, and are enabled to set an example which I feel certain is telling upon the lookers-on. Our congregation, too, all acknowledge, has greatly increased.....

"I cannot tell you how thankful my heart feels for the measure of success we are meeting with. *It is putting new life into my ministerial work,* and I am sure we ought to be greatly obliged to you for recommending John —— and his wife. I scarcely know which of the two is most useful."

Conclusion of the Matter.

CHAPTER XVI.

I WAS visiting one day a poor woman, who lives in a garret in a crowded alley. Curiosity led me to look from the casement at the mass of red buildings and chimney-tops rising one beyond another. To my surprise, I found myself unable to recognise a single street,—all seemed confusion; the fact was, it was a new point of view to me. But that little casement taught me more of the geography of that locality than a hundred walks would have done. Just so one may gain behind the scenes of daily life a truer view of *cause and effect* than many more gifted persons who only throng the public walks.

I met with an extract from a paper written by a clergyman, on the "Methods and Limitations in the repression of Drunkenness among the Poor," the writer of which states, that "drunkenness is a consequence, rather than a cause, of misery,—the effect of wretched homes, starvation, and rags, upon the human frame." He concludes—shall we say logically?—that improvement in these respects must necessarily precede any attempts to spread temperance amongst the people. He would stem the tide of drunkenness by providing large cooking establishments, where cheap and wholesome food may be provided, and by training young girls for cooks, &c.

We hail every improvement in this respect, and it would, indeed, be a great boon if every working man's wife knew how to make home comfortable.

But there are three facts worth considering.

First: A drunkard has no appetite for food. If the best prepared and most wholesome food were placed before him, he would turn from it with loathing. *The drink must first be removed.*

Secondly: We have known too many good, clean, and thrifty wives, whose husbands were drunkards, to believe it is always the want of home comforts which lead into that vice. The *company* and *public-house* are the snare.

Thirdly: When drunkenness has entered a home, robbing it of the husband's earnings, wherewithal shall a wife provide home comforts?

"You have taught us how to make a shilling go the furthest, but what are we to do? Our husbands spend every shilling in drink." And the benevolent authoress of "Ragged Homes, and how to mend them," was touched by the appeal. A Total Abstinence Society was formed by the City Missionary, upon our plan. Mark the results. In seven months one hundred and sixty signatures were taken, Mrs.

Bayley herself signing the pledge for their encouragement. I was present at their monthly tea-drinking on August 6th, when the happy wives thronged to shake hands with me, and to tell me of their changed homes.

The letter from the City Missionary at Notting Dale is so interesting that I insert part of it, for the sake of others to whom it may be useful:—

* * * * * *

"I think it is a duty to inform you that we have taken a leaf from your book, 'Haste to the Rescue.' We had, by the Lord's blessing, been able to accomplish much in the district in the formation of Mothers' Meetings and Ragged Schools, as you are aware from the faithful details in "Ragged Homes, and how to mend them;" but as yet there was not much effected among the men. The fatal leak of drinking water-logged the homes, so that, notwithstanding the improvement in the stewardess and attention to the sails, we made slow way, and often the ships foundered, leaving the fragments of their families to float on the homeless waves.

"We attempted to meet the cases individually, and also by ordinary temperance meetings, but not with success.

"In January last I read your book, and was much struck with the genius of the work, and determined, in the strength of the Lord, to commence a similar one.

"After making the purpose a subject of earnest prayer, I invited seven men who were subject to drinking to meet me, and gave to each a card, containing the hour and place of meeting, without informing them for what purpose. Five came. I provided coffee and buns,—the conversation was familiar and candid, and was sometimes relieved by a reciprocal jest. After tea, we drew round the fire, and one by one each confessed his unhappiness and a desire for a change. I had invited a man to meet them on account of the change in his character three years previous. This man, a fine specimen of a London plasterer, had been in the habit of spending his means, and frequently his sabbaths, in drinking. On one of my sabbath-morning visits in the streets, a few words were blessed to his conviction, and he went that day to a place of worship, and thence became a follower of the Saviour.

"He spoke freely to our guests on this occasion, and told them of the happiness he had enjoyed since he had left off drinking, and had served the Lord. 'But,' said he, 'I never should have been able to keep from drink without prayer, and there is hardly a room that I plaster that I don't pray in.' I then read Ephesians ii., making application, and the plasterer offered prayer, each man kneeling.

"I then made the intended proposal, that each

should sign the pledge, and the declaration was unanimously signed with evident satisfaction.

"It was agreed to meet again in the same place the following week, with permission to add to our number. When I called during the week to invite another man, I observed his wife lift her apron to her eyes, turn her face to the wall, and appear to be in silent prayer.

"On the evening appointed I was a short time alone in the room, but soon heard thick shoes coming up the double stairs; the six of us met with the addition of three, who were introduced with acclamation.

"No refreshment was provided, but an hour was passed in friendly conversation. I then read Isaiah, lv., and a carpenter offered prayer. The third week brought two or three more, and the man whose wife prayed through her tears said, a mate had promised him to be there, and said he would go and fetch him. So, putting on his hat, he left us, and in a few minutes came back, bringing with him his companion, who was particularly violent when drunk. He looked as if he had just come off some feat of rage. He signed the pledge, and calmly knelt in prayer. I read from St. Mark about the leprous man. It was agreed that on the following week we should hold our first lunar tea-meeting. Twelve pledged members were now present, and Mrs. Bayley being made acquainted with the movement, kindly presided at the table, and afterwards read the demoniac, Mark v., and offered prayer.

"The work has gone on steadily, and increasing every week since, Mrs. Bayley being usually present.

". . . . After the second meeting, a man who has a large family went home, and for the first time for six years prayed with his children, and said it was the first time he had been happy for that period.

"The man who was fetched in by his mate proposed that they should meet weekly for prayer. Half-past eight o'clock every Sunday night was fixed upon: and has so much increased, that it has been necessary to remove it to the school-room, and at this hour there has been joy in the presence of the angels over sinners repenting.

"The wife of one man said that for sixteen years she had not the means of keeping her husband's birthday, but now she had made him a currant-cake, to which furniture, apparel, and kindness, are brought to correspond.

"We beg an interest in your prayers, and may the *character* of the work you have initiated increase and abound till every forlorn hope shall be turned to the gate of Refuge!" . . . .

"The worst evils, and the most difficult to remedy, are those which men bring upon themselves."

Why need any working man's home be wretched

or ragged? In ninety-nine cases out of a hundred drunkenness is the cause. How do we know? Because, wherever *that* is taken out of the way, peace and plenty preside. Which, we ask every unprejudiced mind, is the cause,—which the effect?

Dr. Barnes, Fellow of the Royal College of Physicians, in his inaugural address to students in London Hospital Medical School, October 7th, 1860, says, "Turn your eyes for a moment to the Hospital close by. The first patient—sick with fever or consumption—is a victim to malaria, rising up from the sewerage, sodden soil, &c. . . . Further on is one whose energies are destroyed, whose body is diseased, whose mind is debased, by indulgence in those accursed drinks *whose use is abuse, whose purity is foulness, to adulterate which is a superfluous or impossible fraud!*"

Fellow-Christians! the question resolves itself into one of the highest principle—love to perishing sinners for Christ's sake. It is these "accursed drinks" which bind the people in the deadliest chains that Satan ever yet forged.

Will you, *for His sake who "pleased not Himself,"* —*for your weak brother's sake*—discountenance, by example and practice, the lie—fatal to so many thousands of precious souls—that these drinks, "whose use is abuse," are in any degree necessary for health or strength. It is an ascertained fact that

60,000 persons die annually in Great Britain from drunkenness. But this is only a small part of the truth; there are another 60,000 annually sliding out of the ranks of moderate drinkers to swell the lists of mortality for the next year. Will you countenance their sin by remaining in their ranks yourself, because to you there is no personal risk? Will you not rather henceforth make a stand against that which is Satan's strong delusion to slay his millions?

The following letter, received by me when in Edinburgh, from my friend Tom Williams, who has been named before, may reach the hearts of some better than any words of our own on this subject:—

"DEAR MADAM,—Excuse the liberty I take of addressing these few lines to you, hoping that you and Mr. Wightman are well, and I hope enjoying your 'out,' and likewise that we shall see you both safe at home once more. Your absence has not made any alteration in the attendance in the meetings. I think we are as a body still pressing forward through all our difficulties, which are many. The election [*a municipal election*] has made some stir in town, but I have not heard of any of our men falling back.

"It will be five years to-morrow since I was sold up; in fact, I sold myself. . . Oh, the misery I have had since then! . . . Oh! the drunkard's thirst! It was afterwards that I lived on 2*s.* 4½*d.* a-week, which I told you about, when I was five nights in Mr. ——'s barn, and never had my clothes off, and made a beer-barrel of myself. Conscience would sometimes speak. After that I left my family, and became assistant at a public-house, and I was the joy of the house: nobody like Tom, singing songs, telling tales and lies. When my child died conscience spoke again, but the thirst again broke out, and my sorrow was drowned in liquid fire.

"At last I signed the pledge, and became what you see I am, by the grace of God. I have no occasion to turn back. Sometimes, when I think of my past life, I feel ready to give up all for lost, only for *those precious promises of Christ.*

"I hope you will induce some one in Edinburgh to *give up the little drop* for the sake of men like me, and not to take that which causeth their weak brother to stumble. Please excuse the length of this note.

"From your affectionate servant,
"TOM WILLIAMS."

A clergyman once said to me, "I don't call a drunkard a weak *brother;* he is not a brother at all." I ask, has any one looked into the Lamb's book of life? God has many dear children *chosen in Christ before the foundation of the world,* who are not yet brought out of darkness. Even some are in Babylon. "*Come out of her, my people.*" Tom Williams was a sheep, though he was a *lost sheep:* thank God, he is now "*found.*"

There is another appalling fact, not yet named.

There is a transmitted tendency to drunkenness. The children of drunkards can hardly be moderate drinkers,—total abstinence is their only safeguard. Dr. Alexander Peddie says that dipsomania is most frequently visited on children for the sins of their parents, especially when the latter have suffered from repeated attacks of *delirium tremens,* or have been confirmed dipsomaniacs, and it is sometimes met with in their offspring during the years of childhood. He adds, whether it occurs from acquired vicious habits, or from an insane transmitted tendency, "the pathological results and mental phenomena are the same. There is impaired volition, complete loss of self-respect and self-control. The sole desire for existence is to obtain stimulating drinks, and, to gratify for one moment the insane impulse, the victim of it would stake even his eternal welfare."

Dr. Peddie proposes separate asylums and sanitaria of a private nature, but subject to inspection, in which patients who offer themselves should be treated, only so long as they themselves determine; and, with regard to the compulsory patients, he would give the power to the sheriffs to place them under control, at the instance of a friend or public board; of course such power would be watched narrowly, lest it should infringe the liberty of the subject.

But, unless the patient be made to understand that the total relinquishment of all stimulants is the only chance he has of avoiding a relapse, of what use will a temporary residence be in the best asylum in the world?

Again, it is not so much the love of drink as the pleasure of meeting friends which leads the working man into the public-house.

Man is a gregarious being, he cannot live isolated, he loves to meet his fellows, and to have social intercourse with them. If the reckless and ungodly company is given up, he needs other associates who will help him on in his new and untried path of self-denial and honour. It is affecting to see working men in towns standing about in the streets in groups, after working hours, without a place to sit down in, except the tempting and ever-ready ale-bench. If we had a continental climate, it would not matter so much.

I have been distressed in night-visits at cottages, when the whole family were assembled, to see how the entrance of one guest, and that by no means an unwelcome one, has "put them about" to find sitting accommodation.

Now, what a boon a large Common Room would be in towns! We hear of Reading-rooms, Class-rooms, Coffee-rooms, &c., but no one seems to have thought of a Common Room, for social conversation, where working men may sit down with a companion for a friendly chat, and where wages may be paid.

"Before I knew about your Society and the meetings, I didn't know what to do with myself at nights to keep away from the public-house. I used to go and sit for three hours at a time at the railway station watching the trains come in; we want some sort of a place to sit down in, to save going to the public-house." This was said by a man who had eleven children: what space had he at home to meet a friend?

It would not be advisable to have refreshment at the Common Room, because it is better for working men to take their meals at home in the evenings. And when it requires ten or twelve shillings a-week for *bread alone*, when the family is large, how can money be spared for extra luxuries between the meal hours?

We hope to set the example in Shrewsbury, and I would earnestly ask all who are interested in our work to help us by their prayers.

Our Society numbers upwards of a thousand persons, of whom nearly seven hundred are adults. We have no room larger than St. Alkmond's schoolroom to meet in, which holds, when *crammed*, two hundred and twenty; at our "Readings" nearly a hundred go away, unable to get in.

We want a building which shall comprise a

Reading-room, a room for night classes, a Common Room for conversation, and a large Lecture-room, for our weekly meetings. Towards this, there is not one in our ranks who will be backward in giving his share. But no time must be lost.

We want to borrow a large sum, ground being expensive in the town, to begin our new building at once.

With the exception of 37*l.*, given us in sums varying from 2*s.* 6*d.* to 5*l.*, which we have devoted to *the men's sick fund*, we have been independent of all help towards the expenses of our work.

Lastly, we would most strongly protest against all mere secular reformation.

If we did not believe drunkenness to be the chief hindrance in the path of our working brothers to God, we would not make so strenuous an effort against that one vice.

Nothing short of coming to Christ for pardon and life will save any man.

Whatever hinders that must be taken up and cast out of the way (Hos. iv. 11).

Several Societies have arisen after the example of ours. Some of these are conducted entirely on religious principles. We can testify to the fact that prosperity has been given according to the amount of religious teaching. Where the weekly meetings have been secular, and the speeches simply total abstinence addresses, the members relating their own experience of profit and loss, Societies have dwindled, members have not been looked after, and they have gradually fallen back.

We do not care to establish Total Abstinence Societies as an *end;* that is not our object.

We want to bring *sinners to* CHRIST, and for this reason we earnestly desire them to give up "the drink," because it is *the* besetting hindrance of our home heathen to this blessed end.

We do not see any object in *weekly temperance* meetings for those who have signed; they have passed beyond the need of such a help; we desire to bring new members at once into contact with the rich and free Gospel of Jesus Christ. And for this we recommend the *weekly religious* meetings, where, in a kind, affectionate, and familiar way, they shall be taught their need of Christ, and brought to attend the public services of the sanctuary.

Occasional lectures on scientific or common subjects, or on the claims of total abstinence physiologically or pathologically considered, or any other useful and improving topic, would be most valuable; these need not interfere with the *weekly meetings.*

When a poor man signs the pledge, he has a long uphill work before he can "get straight." He has to encounter the jeers and scoffs of former companions, the claims of creditors, especially publicans, who will show him no mercy because he has dared to think for himself and to free himself from their clutches, and the trials of poverty until he is out of debt. Again, he must work hard daily, with the habit of years against him, and the craving for drink haunting him. When all these things are remembered, how tender-hearted and sympathising every Christian ought to be to such a man! Does he not deserve our *respect?* Is he not worthy of all honour?

In that day, when our advantages shall be set in the balance against his, will not the want of sympathy and love on our part, which left a brother or sister to perish, be more hateful in the sight of God than the drunkenness of a poor man whom we might, by a small sacrifice on our side, have led to abandon his besetting sin?

On the subject of drink our language is not stronger than Scripture, or the voice of our Church in her Homilies, A.D. 1623.

> "Who hath woe? who hath sorrow?
> Who hath contentions? who hath babbling?
> Who hath wounds without cause?
> Who hath redness of eyes?
> They that tarry long at the wine;
> They that go to seek mixed wine.
> Look not thou upon the wine when it is red,
> When it giveth his colour in the cup,
> When it moveth itself aright:

At the last it biteth like a serpent,
And stingeth like an adder.
Thine eyes shall behold strange women,
And thine heart shall utter perverse things.
Yea, thou shalt be as he that lieth down in the midst of the sea,
Or as he that lieth upon the top of a mast.
They have stricken me, shalt thou say, and I was not sick;
They have beaten me, and I felt it not:
When shall I awake?
I will seek it yet again."

"Solomon forbiddeth the very sight of wine. Certainly that must needs be very hurtful which biteth and infecteth like a poisonous serpent, whereby men are brought to filthy fornication, which causeth the heart to devise mischief."—*Homily on Intemperance.*

THE LOVE OF MONEY has forced "*the drink*" upon the people of England.

Drunkenness was not the national sin of Israel in the days of our Lord or of the Apostles, or such words as the following would have been as inapplicable as in our own day. "They that be drunken are drunken in the night." "These men are not drunk, as ye suppose, seeing it is but the third hour of the day." But drunkenness, covetousness, and idolatry, were their national sins in the days of Isaiah and Jeremiah, and they brought God's anger upon the nation before the captivity, and on account of these sins God left them, in judgment, to the sin of *blindness.* (See Isa. xxviii., xxix.)

We, therefore, as patriots and Christians, protest against our national sin in unmeasured terms.

It is the truest charity to do so, for souls are perishing thereby.

It is the truest patriotism to do so, for it is written,

"Righteousness exalteth a nation, but sin is a reproach unto any people."

www.ingramcontent.com/pod-product-compliance
Lightning Source LLC
LaVergne TN
LVHW010228110826
845151LV00004B/1226

* 9 7 8 1 4 2 5 5 2 5 6 1 3 *